Price Hill Saloons

AND MUCH, MUCH MORE!

Larry "Froggy" Schmolt

Published by Edgecliff Press
in partnership with the
Price Hill Historical Society & Museum
Cincinnati, Ohio

Price Hill Saloons and Much, Much More!

By Larry Schmolt

Published by Edgecliff Press, LLC.,
in Partnership with
the Price Hill Historical Society & Museum
Cincinnati, Ohio

www.edgecliffpress.com
www.pricehill.org

ISBN 978-0-9844622-7-8
Library of Congress Control Number 2011927890
© 2011 Larry Schmolt

10 9 8 7 6 5 4 3 2 1

Published in the United States of America

DEDICATION

This book is dedicated to Lee (Toots) Schmolt, along with all the other devoted housewives throughout the Price Hill area. These particular housewives served their husbands supper and then allowed them to go to the nearest saloon after a busy day, to alleviate their tensions.

As the husbands headed for the door, the housewives always reminded them not to forget their "jugs." The housewives knew that they would return with the jugs half full. By then, with the dishes done and the children tucked in their beds, it would be time for those housewives to relax, each with a nice cold glass of beer.

The Price Hill Historical Society & Museum,
a nonprofit educational institution, gratefully
acknowledges the financial assistance of
Judge Norman A. Murdock and his family
in their underwriting support
of this publication.

Photographs are from the collection of the
Price Hill Historical Society & Museum.

Cartoons by Frank W. Egner
from the collection of the
Price Hill Historical Society,
donated by William Bosse.

Newspaper articles reprinted with permission
of the Cincinnati Enquirer, the Price Hill News,
and the Price Hill Press.

Cover design by Roy Hotchkiss
Book design by Julie Hotchkiss

FOREWORD

Over the years, Price Hill, more than any other suburb of the Queen City, was blessed with a large number of saloons. Many Germans, Irish, and other nationalities could find a place to congregate and talk about the news of the day while drinking beer, their favorite beverage. The ownership of these saloons was usually passed down from generation to generation. That was also the case for those who frequented these establishments— sons following in their fathers' footsteps to the nearest welcoming watering hole.

Most of those folks who operated these saloons were the most generous individuals, supporting amateur sports, school and church affairs, and the like. If it wasn't for these saloons, the Hill could not have gained fame for having more building and loan operations than any place in the United States, because many of these financial establishments got their start with a gathering of like-minded fellows in the rear rooms of saloons.

While writing this book, we were approached by many people who had their own favorite saloon stories. Some of the stories were about parents and grandparents who only enjoyed their drinks at their favorite saloons. These stories would have filled several books.

With this in mind, we hope that you will write down your stories about your favorite saloons, for your own family history. We also encourage you to share the stories with the Price Hill Historical Society. We might publish some of the stories in our newsletter and we definitely would like to preserve them in our archives. Maybe, someday, we will be able to publish a second edition about the drinking establishments on the Hill entitled *Heard Around the Saloons of Price Hill*.

Again, it has been fun putting this book together over the past year. Please do not take everything as "gospel." When the old mind has been around for more than eighty years, sometimes certain memories are a little hazy. I tried to recall and relate my memories in the most enjoyable manner for you, the reader.

Larry Schmolt

ACKNOWLEDGMENTS

A special thanks to Mr. Norman Murdock! His generous donation made it possible for the Price Hill Historical Society to publish this book.

Without the Society's archives, this book would not be possible. Thus, I want to give a big thanks to Flo Sparks and Joyce Meyer for their work in the Society's library. Also, thanks to all the others who keep things running day to day: Betty Wagner, Valda Moore, Janice Chaney, Richard Jones, Earl Pitstick, Roy Hotchkiss, and Julie Hotchkiss. And, especially, thank you to all who submitted articles and pictures, which will be preserved in this book and in our library. Please take the time someday soon to visit the Price Hill Historical Society and Museum!

CONTENTS

WHERE IT ALL BEGAN

Long before the boundaries of Cincinnati stretched beyond the Mill Creek, Storrs Township stretched west from the Mill Creek until it met Delhi Township, near where Elder High School sits. The portion of the township near the basin of the Hill, which we now call Lower Price Hill (formerly the Eighth and State area), was a beehive of activity in the mid-1800s. Factories and building supply yards dotted the banks of the Mill Creek. Many wagons pulled by teams of horses were hauling building materials up the steep face of what would eventually become known as Price Hill. Soon houses and businesses were springing up along the streets of the Hill. The Irish and German immigrants who worked in the area, along with the teamsters driving the wagons, had a thirst for their favorite beverage. The Irish loved their whiskey and the Germans, their beer.

A popular spot to quench their thirst was a saloon located at West Eighth and Depot Streets. The saloon was known as Depot Saloon because the horse car barns were located across West Eighth Street. One can visualize this old-time saloon having a mahogany front and rear bar. The rear shelves were lined with the finest whiskey of the day and the bartender was always ready to draw you a cold beer for a nickel. To the rear was the free lunch counter loaded with all kinds of goodies to fill a hungry workman's appetite. Yes, one only had to purchase a nice beer to avail him of the free lunch, but the barkeeper was betting that one would linger awhile and purchase quite a few beers. The saloon keeper's wife, who usually lived upstairs above the bar and did all the cooking, kept the lunch counter well-stocked with food throughout the lunch hour.

In later years, the name of the bar was changed to Christoph's Café and Grill. By that time the free lunch had gone, but food was served throughout the day at a very nominal cost. During these years, what made this saloon so popular was its location at a crossroads to the western side of town. Four streetcars passed by the intersection of Eighth and State, where many passengers transferred to a car going to other locations. A great many of

A Lower Price Hill bar

these passengers worked in the factories operating in the area, as well as factories along State or Spring Grove Avenues. Added to this were the many railyards that were in the area. Three o'clock was the closing time for most banks but it was also the time that many railroaders who passed through the area would get off work. All these workers were eager to get their paychecks cashed before making their way home, and with the banks already closed, Christoph's provided the service of cashing those checks. They charged a fee of only a few pennies from each check. For example, if your check was for $15.49, the charge for cashing it was the four odd pennies. On some days they would probably handle more cash than a lot of banks in town.

Of course, any good barkeeper would know that he could not operate his business on making a few pennies on each check. He was betting that you were going to stay around for a few beers. Better yet, since it was payday, you might even have a shot of whiskey from the top shelf.

Christoph's was bought by Gus Kurlas, and he renamed the place the Gus Kurlas Café. Then suddenly, the streetcars were no more. Automobiles took over and Eighth and State saw fewer and fewer people transferring at this location. Businesses relocated and the saloon business fell off. People frequenting the saloons were less friendly than they had been in the old days. Many were prone to getting loud and boisterous after having a few too many drinks. Fights and the like became common at the saloons. As business got worse, someone even ended up getting killed during one of those fights at the Gus Kurlas Café, once a glorious old saloon. Not knowing how to dispose of the body, the guilty parties decided that under the concrete floor of the basement would make a good grave. Through the good work of the police and the evidence of fresh concrete covering the burial place, the body was discovered and the perpetrators were brought to justice. What an eerie way for one of the west side's first saloons to come to a close!

In the heyday of the neighborhood at the foot of Price Hill, there was even a bowling alley with a café which operated successfully in the area. It was located at South and Depot Streets, just opposite a firehouse on the other corner. Many firefighters of the day were famous for pretending to go over "to get a sandwich for their lunch." A few were known to sneak a beer while waiting to be served. One of the most notable was Captain Beiler, who was the captain of the Ladder Company. Upon retiring, he purchased the saloon. The bowling alley had already closed. He said that as a fireman he had gone into the saloon so often, it only would be right that he retire there. The building was torn down long ago, however, and only an empty lot remains.

> *Fun Fact*: In 1892, the output of beer in Cincinnati was close to a million and a half barrels, thus showing the enormous growth of the brewing industry in the city. The residents of the city consumed 815,000 barrels of this amount. The average consumption per person was fifty gallons (the population at that time was about 500,000), pouring close to ten million dollars into the economy. One can see what beer meant to Cincinnati in those days.

My favorite bar is the Sportsman Bar, because it has stood the test of time and is still in operation. I like the term "Sportsman." I think the only thing for years that was ever sporting about it was the bookie writing sheets in the backroom. Yes, you could bet that when it came time for the Kentucky Derby and you had a hunch on a horse, you could always go into the Sportsman, have a beer, and someone would take your bet to the backroom for you.

I always thought it was great that you could look east on the Eighth Street Viaduct and see the streetcar coming, in case you were waiting to transfer from the crosstown car to the Elberon or Warsaw line. You would have just enough time to run into the Sportsman Bar. The bartender, who was always accommodating, would pour you a fast one, which you could gulp down quickly and run out in time to catch your streetcar. Also, if it was late at night and you were hungry but the kitchen was closed, you could smell the onions on the grill from the Krystal Kitchen next door. Who could resist a few hamburgers before heading for home? Or, if you cared to walk up to the corner, you could enjoy one of the "Hoppy's" hot tamales. For years, his little cart was a fixture at this location. But most of all, if you had lingered too long and had a few "too many" and Mamma was waiting supper for you, it was best to make a quick stop at Nick Jovannes Sweet Shop to bring her home a box of his famous chocolate candy. Most of these old saloons and the other businesses are gone, but the memories linger on.

TOP OF THE HILL

Research indicates that few saloons dotted the Hill in the mid-1800s. At that time the roads to Price Hill were difficult to navigate. Today's Glenway Avenue was then known as Glen's Way, as it led to the hamlet of Glen Grove. The street was full of ruts from the wheels of the buggies that made their way along the road, which was also dotted with several toll stations. The keepers of these toll stations usually kept the road in repair and in some cases used wood planks to cover holes in the road. The Sisters of Charity at Mount Saint Vincent Convent, now Seton High School, would often refer to the road as "Plank Road."

In 1887, the Village of Warsaw was the largest settlement on the Hill. The businesses in operation at this time included Clark's Carpenter Shop, the William Laber Tavern (also known as "Pap's"), Andrew Zoller Sr.'s tavern, the village blacksmith, Hermann's Smithy and Wagon Shop, and the Kreis Homestead and Winery. During this time the Cincinnati-Warsaw-Brookville Pike extended clear to Brookville, Indiana.

Mostly farmers from Delhi Township, along with others from Indiana, used the road. They would haul their produce to market in downtown Cincinnati. Since there were many horse stables in the city, they were most likely to haul a load of manure back to

Bender's Saloon, at Glenway and Iliff

the farm on their return trip. The farmers relied on the Village of Warsaw for various things. The village blacksmith was a place they could stop on their return trip to check the shoes of their horses or maybe even take care of repairs to their wagons. It only seemed natural to stop by William Laber's Tavern for a beer and a "shooter" while waiting for these repairs. This tavern was located at the corner of Glenway and Second Street, which is now Iliff Avenue. This same location later became Bender's Saloon until sometime into the 1920s. The saloon was then closed, and it became the location of one of the first drug stores on the Hill. Recently the building was torn down.

Another favorite tavern of this era was Haberstumpf's Five Mile Tavern. Records indicate that this was located at the corner of Glenway and Winfield Avenues. We know from the telephone book of 1902 that the Haberstumpfs also operated a tavern in downtown Cincinnati on Walnut Street. They were most famous for their gardens, at the corner of Glenway and Rutledge Avenues, where the Germans held many of the Schutzenfest celebrations (similar to that of today's Kolping Society).

Many can remember that the Warsaw car line turned at this point for years, which was known as the "Carson Loop." One can only imagine the dancing, drinking, and music that went on at this location on any given Sunday in the summer.

Funeral corteges making their way to the cemeteries on the Hill chose to make the steeper climb up Warsaw Avenue. About half way up the Hill, between Wilder and Grand Avenues, was a curve in the road, as well as a huge tree hanging over it. This became the site where funeral processions usually stopped to rest their horses and became known as "dead man's curve." Then, as they made their way out Warsaw, they'd turn at "Cemetery Road," which is now Enright Avenue. When they approached Eighth Street, the German Cemetery was located to the south and the Irish Cemetery to the north, with Mause's Tavern on

7

Streetcar #36 at Carson Loop

the northeast corner. After burying the dead, it was only right for them to go drown their sorrows at the tavern. One can only imagine how rowdy things might have gotten when both the Irish and Germans had a burial on the same day. Is it any wonder that Mr. Mause had to build a garden out back to keep the two groups separated? One thing for sure is that the Irish filled their cemetery much faster than the Germans. It became necessary to open a new cemetery further out West Eighth Street to accommodate new burials. To this day, however, the Germans continue to bury their dead at the original location.

The founder of our neighborhood, Rees Price, realized that the face of Price Hill was too steep for the many wagons hauling his building materials (he owned a lumberyard and stone quarry

east of the Mill Creek) up for the new houses being built, so his sons, William and John, built an inclined plane up the face of the hill. It was built not only to carry passengers (which most inclines were doing), but also to carry horses and wagons of freight. About the time the Price Hill Incline was being built, St. Lawrence Parish was formed. The parish was made up of many German immigrants who had a great thirst for their beer and the need for saloons to provide it.

The following paragraph is an excerpt from the 125th Anniversary booklet *Saint Lawrence, Mother Church of Price Hill:*

> Among the Catholic churches are St. Lawrence at St. Lawrence Corner. The Rev. J. W. Bonner and the Rev. H. J. Richter founded the parish and the first building was dedicated in 1870. The present church building, started as a basement chapel, was dedicated in 1894. Its school is one of the largest parochial schools in the city. St. William Church and School, West Eighth and Sunset, were dedicated in 1910. Its beautiful windows, with symbolic designs, are unmatched in the city. Holy Family Church was dedicated in 1914, its area having been divided with that of St. Lawrence Parish in 1884.

Price Hill definitely had its share of Catholic residents, as more and more parishes were formed on the Hill. But in these earliest days, there weren't any church festivals yet, so what did Mr. Price do for those beer-thirsty German Catholic residents of the Hill? Not only did he build the Price Hill Incline, he also built a giant hall for dancing and celebrating, which was known as the Price Hill House. But this hall would be much different from those at the top of other inclines. Being opposed to drinking, Price prohibited alcohol products from being consumed on the premises; thus Price Hill became known as "Buttermilk Hill."

One can only imagine the reaction of some German friends visiting from out of town. Envision taking them up the Hill on the Incline, sitting back to enjoy the view and the cool breezes on a hot day, only to be told that the strongest drink available is a glass of buttermilk. As they sit there **not** enjoying their drink, they can hear music and cheer coming from the Bellevue House across the valley. Not only does the Bellevue House serve beer, they even have their own brewery on the premises.

Is it any wonder an entrepreneur named Hock chose to open a saloon directly across from the exit at the top of the Incline? George Hock began selling beer and ran advertisements proclaiming that his saloon was at the "Top of the Price Hill Incline." Over the years one has to wonder how many people walked over

to Mr. Hock's place thinking it was the Price Hill House, to the dismay of Mr. Price.

The Price Hill House on "Buttermilk Hill" had a grand veranda that seated a thousand diners. As they ate and sipped their buttermilk and soft drinks, they could look out over the beautiful Ohio Valley. However, the operation proved not to be profitable, and the establishment closed at the turn of the century. Someone else took it over and began to serve alcoholic beverages, but it only attracted Price Hill folks and a few from out of town who knew its past history. It operated as a summer garden until 1932, when it closed.

The building then sat vacant for several years before becoming an American Legion Post. The last occupant was the Price Hill Church of the Nazarene. In the early 1940s, it was torn down, and today a radio tower occupies the spot where the Price Hill House once stood.

PROMINENT SALOONS
ON THE HILL

One of the most prominent saloons of the old times had to be Joe Brauer's Saloon, located at the corner of Warsaw and McPherson Avenues. One could say that his saloon played an important role in the ownership of many homes that were built on the Hill throughout the years. The rear room of this saloon was where the former Price Hill Electric Building and Loan was organized. In fact, the safe of the saloon was used to keep the money of the organization for years.

If you were building a house in the early days of the neighborhood, you met with the directors on the night they were having their meeting and they would approve your loan on the spot. It was nothing like today, when you have to wait a long time for them to make up their minds. The Price Hill Electric Building and Loan later became the United Savings Association and began making loans to many of the grandchildren whose families had borrowed from the former business. United Savings Association built a new building further out on Glenway, but after many years at this location, they went out of business and the building is now the home of the Covedale Library.

Mr. Brauer was one of the kindest men anyone would ever want to meet. No one in need ever went into his place without Joe giving them some money to help them out. But as with many saloons, Prohibition hit his establishment hard. His granddaughter, in later years, noticed that there was a soda fountain in the saloon. She asked him what the fountain was for and he replied, "It was a way to feed the family when I could not sell alcohol."

As a youngster, I can remember going into the saloon for a hamburger. He had a little hot plate stove by the front window. He would throw a hamburger patty in the skillet. When it was done, he'd put a big slice of onion on it and put it between two slices of rye bread. The juice would just run out as you bit into it. Believe me, it was nothing like what McDonald's puts out today and calls a hamburger.

Joseph Brauer's Saloon

Joe had three sons, two of whom followed him into the saloon business after serving their country in World War I. Both sons learned from their father to make the same kind of great hamburger and to be the nicest gentlemen anyone would ever want to meet.

During all the years he operated the saloon, he never owned the building. In later years he thought of buying the building, but changed his mind due to its deteriorated condition. His son, Ben, operated the saloon along with him. When Joe did retire, Ben took over the business but moved to a building at Warsaw and Wells Avenues.

The barkeep's namesake, his son Joe, decided to strike out on his own and opened a pool hall further up on Warsaw Avenue. After several years, he decided to move to a location on Enright Avenue. His previous Warsaw Avenue location became the home of Charlie Yeager's Price Hill Paint and Glass. The location on Enright Avenue was eventually torn down and became the location of the present Price Hill Post Office.

What a treat it was for a youngster to go into the pool hall on Enright and watch some of the best pool sharks on the Hill! We would sit there with a bottle of Union orange pop, trying not to make a sound. Any noise could cause one of the pool players to miss a shot or scratch. We knew that would result in receiving a dirty stare and having to leave. I can still visualize the wires, running above each table, with a string of beads used by the players to keep score.

The Ballinasloe Café, located at the corner of Glenway and Purcell Avenues, was another saloon that has survived the test of time. It is not clear when this establishment first opened, but it sure must not have been at the present location when the great flood of Price Hill occurred. Since it is located directly below where the water towers ruptured, it surely would have been washed away. You see, there were four 48-foot-high steel tanks located on the hill above Glenway between Considine and Purcell Avenues. On June 29, 1881, a tank gave way, and suddenly a wall of water enveloped the land below, washing away all in its path. The land where the water tanks had stood became a park, and over the years we always called the park "The Tanks" or "Tank Park," but many of us never knew why.

Ballinasloe's Café was later renamed Coney's Café and was operated by two brothers, Frank and Harry. As word had it, they were as different as night and day. Harry was the nice guy, and Frank, who lived above the saloon with his family, was not so nice. One thing for sure was that if he didn't like you, he let you know in a hurry. When ordering a beer he would say, "You

Coney's Cafe, formerly Ballinasloe's

don't live around here, do you, no sir. Well, don't ask for another beer!" It was a way of saying, drink up and don't come back again. Over the years it remained a neighborhood family saloon. Today, the saloon remains in operation but has had many different owners over the past years.

Hartung's Cafe, Glenway Avenue

Maybe we have saved the best of old-time saloons for last. The best would have to be Hartung's Saloon at Glenway and McKeone Avenues. One could probably write an entire book on this saloon, but I will limit it to a couple of pages. Al Hartung, father to Bob, started the business, and after his death it was only natural that Bob became the owner. Prohibition and the stock market crash had hit them hard. Bob always said that Coke had a lot to do with Prohibition coming about, so the one thing that was never served at Hartung's was this product. Anyone who patronized the saloon usually knew not to ask for it because they would be told, "Don't let the door hit you as you leave," and he really meant it! This was probably one of the few stag saloons in the city. Someone once asked how you knew it was a stag bar. The answer was that they only had one bathroom.

The only lady who was welcome at Hartung's was Maureen Bonfield, who ran the Crow's Nest on West Eighth Street. Each year she would bring a birthday cake to Bob and they would reminisce about the old times they had when they were both classmates at St. William School.

This building was also home to the Liars' Club, which met once a month. The dues were one dollar per month. For this dollar, you got all you could eat and drink, thanks to the generosity of Bob. Over the years they supported many charitable causes and usually donated money at their Christmas party for some needy family. Nick Dumas, a mailman, would always do the cooking and see that there was plenty to eat. Nick had been an old huckster and could not get selling fruits and vegetables out of his blood after becoming a mailman. On any given day, the rear table would be loaded with a display of his produce. Best of all was when he made turtle soup and bottled it in quart jars.

ANNOUNCING
OPENING - OF

HARTUNG'S
CAFE

Tomorrow
Saturday, July 1

Beer and ALE

ON TAP 5c and 10c

4400 GLENWAY AVE.   Near Carson School

THE HARTUNG LIARS' CLUB *were in the news in 1974 when the group donated money raised at a dance for an athletic program at Santa Maria Neighborhood House. At that time, Jake Riddle was the current president of the Hartung Liar's Club and James Mathews was past president.*

Many stories have come out of Hartung's, but one of the best was that Bob did not have much love for banks. Thus he usually kept large sums of money hidden throughout the saloon. One of the regulars came in one day and had just sold his house for a sum of around fifteen thousand dollars. He still had the check for that amount with him. In a kidding manner he said that if Bob could cash the check, he would buy the house a drink. Unbeknownst to him, Bob had heard his declaration. Suddenly Bob disappeared behind the bar and upon reappearing, came back with huge stacks of money, with rubber bands around them and began counting out the fifteen thousand dollars. This poor guy's face got as red as fire as Bob handed him a brown bag to stuff his cash in. "I'll have a double off the top shelf," were the last words the guy heard from most everyone in the bar. From that day on, the "regulars" learned not to mention money in front of Bob. The guy who had just sold his house and walked out with his bag of cash and his tail between his legs was a good example of why one should keep one's mouth shut!

It was well known throughout the city that this saloon was not the cleanest. This fact was also well known at City Hall, due to the large number of police and firefighters who frequented the place. Politicians would show their faces, often knowing that the crowd who went there always showed up at the polls on Election Day. One notable was the Venerable Judge Al Luebbers, who lived several blocks up off Glenway. Usually he would take his nightly walk with a stop at Hartung's to smoke a cigar, have a few beers, a chat with the boys, and enjoy his nightly visit with everyone.

Even though the place was not air-conditioned, the regulars knew better than to turn on the fan on a hot summer night for fear it would cause a dust storm. Over the years, health inspectors bypassed the location, knowing it was useless to try and have it cleaned. Those who frequented the saloon knew its condition. If they cared to drink in a place such as it was, why bother them?

Then a new inspector from the other side of town was transferred to the area so that Hartung's was in his jurisdiction. He boasted to his fellow workers that he would get the place cleaned up. Thus he stopped by and began inspecting. After finishing, he had a list of violations a mile long. He handed the list to Bob and told him to have them taken care of by the following week, when he would return. As usual, Bob stuck the list of violations in the drawer and went about playing gin rummy, which he loved to do when the night bartender arrived.

The next week the inspector was back, as promised. He asked how many of the orders had been complied with. Bob pulled the list from the drawer and said he really had not gotten around to them yet. The inspector was so mad that he ordered Bob to close down immediately. Bob replied that would happen after his customers finished their drinks, and with that the inspector left. Riding by several days later, the inspector saw some cars in front of the saloon. He went up and noticed the door was locked but a bunch of people were standing around. When someone let the inspector in, everyone grabbed a broom, a mop, or a rag. The inspector was furious that the place was supposed to be closed and that there were so many drinks on the bar. Bob just looked at him and said, "There isn't anything wrong with giving my help a drink while they work here, is there?"

The inspector, angered at his comment, immediately said that he would call the police. Bob in turn replied, "No need to do that; there are four or five of them here helping me. "

With that the inspector headed back to the office and asked his supervisor to assign him to a different district.

Bob was one of the most generous people anyone would ever want to meet. If some organization, such as the March of Dimes or the like, placed a can on the bar for donations, when they came back to pick up the can, he would ask them to let him see that can. He would shake the can and usually say, "Don't seem like donations were too good." Then he would reach in his pocket and pull out a twenty and place it in the can. While trick-or-treating on Halloween, kids always made sure Hartung's Saloon was one of their stops, because they always knew he would be giving out nickel candy bars and great big red apples.

But eventually, Bob's health began to deteriorate, making it almost impossible for him to continue to run the bar, so his two bartenders continued to run the business until Bob finally passed away. It was thought that the family would sell the saloon to Vic Moss, who for the past years had been loyal to Bob. But they

decided that they did not want the place to operate anymore and one Sunday afternoon all the regulars assembled for one last drink. A lot of tears were shed that day.

For several years the saloon remained closed and Bob's nephew, who was a firefighter, quit his job and took on the challenge of running a saloon, calling it "The Other Hartung." He, along with his wife, opened the kitchen and began serving food. But as many before them had discovered, the saloon business wasn't for everyone, and it soon closed.

Then, of all things—I felt for sure that Bob was rolling over in his grave—a restaurant called Ferdinand's opened in the old Hartung's building. They said they served the best authentic Mexican food in town, but the Germans of the Hill must not have had a taste for that kind of food. Maybe Ferdinand's was a little before their time because it also soon closed. And so a saloon, which over the years was such an icon on the Hill, became just a memory.

Rees E. Price

Our founder, Rees E. Price, may not have liked those who consumed alcohol, but his Price Hill Incline sure made it easier for a bunch of Germans (who loved their beer) and Irish (with their taste for whiskey) to build their homes up on Price's Hill. Before the Incline, a team of horses pulling a wagon could only make two trips up the Hill each day with loads of building materials. Now that they could use the Incline, they could increase the number of loads one team could transport to four each day.

Many prominent city folks were eager to trade the foul air of the city's basin for the clean air of the Hill, and houses began to spring up all over Price Hill. To quench their thirst, saloons also started to appear in record numbers. By 1880 there were over two thousand saloons throughout the Cincinnati area. Some of the local breweries even began to open their own saloons or

U.S. IS VOTED DRY
36th STATE RATIFIES DRY AMENDMENT

provide money for a saloonkeeper to go into business. Competition became so fierce for customers that many saloons had a free lunch counter—I have already mentioned the free lunch at the Depot Saloon. So, by purchasing a beer you could help yourself to the delicacies that were on the counter, which had often been prepared by the wife of the saloonkeeper.

Many Price Hill saloons opened in this era. It is hard to determine by records when some of the saloons I've mentioned first opened, but all are thought to have been in existence before passage of the Volstead Act—Prohibition—on October 28, 1919.

John Doll's Saloon was located at West Eighth and Overlook. The area around the New St. Joseph Cemetery at the end of West Eighth Street began to develop as burials in the old Irish Cemetery were no longer possible. We assume that many a drink was consumed in Doll's saloon after the Irish buried their dead. The

John Doll's Saloon on West Eighth Street

Doll's Saloon, interior

building where the saloon once was is still standing. Today it is home to a beauty salon. One could say, "from saloon to salon!"

Later, when bowling became a popular pastime, a bowling alley was added in the rear of Doll's Saloon. Then ownership was turned over to the Boeing family, who later turned the saloon into a grocery store during Prohibition. The location of the Doll Saloon was next door to where Curnayn's Tavern now stands.

Just down the street from Doll's, the Crow's Nest is located at West Eighth Street and Nebraska Avenue, or should we say

The Crow's Nest Cafe

Interior of the Crow's Nest Cafe in the late 1800s

"at the end of the Elberon car line." It is yet another saloon that has stood the test of time. The odd thing being is that it has come full circle since it first was opened by the Crowe family — Glenn O'Dell, the present owner, is a relative of the original owners.

Located opposite the cemetery, many have drowned their sorrows here over the years after burying a dearly departed one. I always got a kick out of the sign which for years hung on the wall saying, "If you think things are dead here, just look out the window across the street." As with the Mueller Saloon, the Crow's Nest had a ball field in the rear for years. I guess some lively games were played there when the two teams got together, regardless of whose field they were using.

After the Crowe's gave up ownership, the Horaks bought the saloon and renamed it Horak's Night Club. It was a place to go on a Saturday night, to listen to a band, and do a little dancing. But the most famous thing that happened during the Horaks' ownership was that they began to serve a chicken dinner on Sunday afternoons. People would flock to the saloon for the dinner. Many customers came by streetcar to visit the graves of their departed and made it a ritual to have a good chicken dinner at Horak's afterwards.

The Crow's Nest Bar, circa 1890

With the passing of the Horaks, Kiestie Bonfield and his wife, Maureen, took over ownership of the Crow's Nest. Kiestie had many friends throughout the Hill, and on any given night, many politicians would frequent the location. But most of all, the fame of the saloon increased in this period with the appearance of the Schaeffer family, who were very talented musicians. With their sing-a-longs, they would pack the place on any given Friday or Saturday night. The best time was when St. Patrick's Day came around and the sidewalks were filled with green sawdust. The green beer and good times would flow from early in the morning until way past midnight. Kiestie passed away far too young and the job of running the saloon became Maureen's. Trying to raise a young family by herself and running a saloon was just too much of a task for her, and she was forced to sell the saloon.

Along came the Hassett family. Big Jim had been a firefighter for some thirty or so years, and he was ready to begin a new

profession as saloonkeeper. So, with his sons, Jim and Pat, the Hassett family took over the ownership of the saloon. Their first project was to refurbish the second floor, which had sat vacant for sometime, and turn it into a hall for parties. Both Jim and Pat had played sports at Elder High School, so they were well known throughout the area. Many of their old friends frequented the saloon. In addition, many of Big Jim's friends from the fire department not only frequented the saloon, but hosted many of their retirement parties in the upstairs party room.

Big Jim loved to go hunting for deer in Colorado each year, so one of his deer head trophies hung over the bar. He would always like to kid around with any youngster who came into the saloon. He would tell them that the deer ran through the wall, but only got his head through. He would then take the youngster to the room behind the bar to show them the rest of the deer. The youngster, believing the tale, would think that the deer was still there. Only when the youngster saw a blank wall in the other room did he would realize he'd been snookered.

After operating the saloon for several years, the Hassett boys finally realized, as mentioned repeatedly, that the saloon business is not the easiest job in the world. So they went on to other pursuits and sold the business.

Over the next few years two sisters, Helen and Zola, tried to operate the saloon. They sold to Pat Emmett, who sold to Peggy Maue. Peggy had been president of the Price Hill Civic Club for a number of years and had made many friends throughout the Hill. When she took over the operation of the Crow's Nest, there was a strong demand to bring Price Hill Day back to the Hill — it had been held at Stricker's Grove for many years.

With this in mind, the area around the saloon was chosen as the locale for a street fair to celebrate the heritage of the Hill. The event was called "Party on the Hill" and bands were brought in along with street vendors. "Party on the Hill" began in 1998 and lasted for five years. It became too much work for volunteers and in some years resulted in very little profit.

Meanwhile, Peggy, like other saloonkeepers before her, found that running a saloon could become a very trying business. Then, as I've already mentioned, Glen O'Dell bought the Crow's Nest and continues to operate the bar and restaurant as a very successful business to this day.

Moeller's Grill and Beer Garden at 5301 Glenway Avenue oddly began not only as a saloon, but a gas station and lubritorium in 1910. One thing for sure was that there probably was not much business from automobiles in those days. So what better way to pass the time of day than by serving up a few beers? Harry J. and George Moeller wrote a tribute to their father in the Price Hill Historical Society's newsletter, *Heritage on the Hill,* and gave permission to reprint it in this book.

MOELLER'S GRILL AND BEER GARDEN

By George Moeller

The three-story brick building that housed Moeller's Grill on Glenway Avenue was built around 1910 by Mr. Tom Ware, mainly to accommodate the C & O Railroad employees who worked in the roundhouse on the steam engines at the railroad yard at Glenway and Boudinot Avenues (now Glencrossing Shopping Center). Mr. Ware had a bar, a gas station, and a lubritorium in the building at 5301 Glenway Avenue.

During World War I, while many men were away, the 18th Amendment was passed, which prohibited the sale of alcoholic beverages. This law gave rise to gangs, bootleggers, and a high crime rate. "Prohibition," as it was called, lasted for 15 years. It wasn't until the Congress repealed Prohibition in 1933 that alcohol sales again became legal.

Moeller's Grill

One of the first people in this area to receive a legal license to sell alcoholic beverages was Harry Moeller, Sr. In 1933, he and his wife Anna started Moeller's Rathskeller at Harding and Glenmore Avenues in Cheviot, Ohio. In 1936, Mr. Ware, knowing that Mr. Moeller was a stellar performer in his field, asked him to come to Price Hill and fill a vacancy in his establishment. He accepted the challenge and brought his wife, Anna, and their three sons, Harry Jr., Charles, and George, along with him to live in the apartment above the business. Mr. Ware continued to operate the gas station, while Mr. Moeller took over the operation of the bar and grill.

Almost immediately, a great transformation took place at Mr. Ware's establishment on Glenway Avenue. A new kitchen was built in the rear of the existing building. In the barroom, a new bar, steam table, and cash register were also added. To take advantage of the beautiful mature trees on the grounds in the rear, a magnificent beer garden took shape. Trees were whitewashed, tan bark was put on the grounds, and a bandstand was built for Mr. Joe Colnot and his orchestra. The beer garden was enclosed with a wooden picket-type fence, with colored lights strung all around. It truly was a lovely, fun place to be in the good old summertime in Cincinnati.

World War II brought with it many changes. The Moeller family's two eldest sons, Harry Jr. and Charles, served in the U.S. Army Air Corps during the war. Charles, stationed in Panama, contracted polio and soon died of the disease. Harry Sr. and a devoted employee, Mr. Paul Robisch, carried much of the load of running the bar and grill during the war years (1942–1945). It was in 1955 that Harry Sr. decided to retire and gave the business to his remaining two sons, Harry Jr. and George. They continued to operate the bar, grill, and pony keg for 31 more years, until it was sold in 1986, so that they too could retire.

It was the end of an era when Moeller's Grill closed after 50 years of operation (1936–1986). The building was razed and is now the site of one of Dr. Wing's Eye Care locations.

John Mueller's Roadhouse and Restaurant — not to be confused with Moeller's Grill — was located at the corner of Glenway and Cleves-Warsaw Pike. The spot is now occupied by Fifth/Third Bank. What a grand old saloon this must have been in its hey-day. It was pos-sibly frequented by farmers in the area as they made their way with their crops down Glenway Avenue. As we look at the old picture, it is also possible that with all the rooms above the saloon, some may have

Mueller's Roadhouse

Baseball at Mueller's

spent the night here. Located to the rear of the saloon was a ballfield. One can only imagine the hollering and shouting that went on here as neighboring teams played one another. Following the game, they would retire to the saloon for some liquid refreshments. The area once occupied by the ballfield is now lined with many fine houses on a street which bears the name Relleum Avenue. If you notice, Mueller spelled in reverse is Relleum, in tribute to Mr. Mueller.

BREWERIES

Where was all this beer coming from that was being consumed on Price Hill? With over 225 breweries in the Cincinnati area, not one existed on Price Hill. That is not to say that during Prohibition a lot of beers were not brewed in the homes of some of the Germans who had built large homes on the Hill. But the closest commercial brewery near the Hill was a small one in Sedamsville that produced less than a thousand barrels in any given year. It was know as the Reuter and Betting Brewery. Just down the Hill on Quebec Avenue in Fairmount was the Becker Brewing Company, which for over the years was said to have produced some of the finest lager beers around.

Over the years the brewing industry poured much into the economy of the Cincinnati area. Looking back at figures from 1894, local consumers spent about ten million dollars on the consumption of beer. To produce this much beer, it was necessary to use over a million and a half bushels of malt and hops. When one thinks about this time, there were no trucks to haul these materials from the farm to the brewery. Just think of the number of horses, wagons, and the drivers that had to be employed. After the brewing process, the by-products had to be disposed of, usually by being fed to cattle or hogs. Is it any wonder that Cincinnati was known as Porkopolis?

To work in one of these breweries was a much sought-after job for many of the Germans who had come over from the old country. The brewmeister, who was considered the king of the brewery, was paid a salary ranging from $7,500 to $15,000 per year. A common laborer was getting $1.50 per day plus all the beer they could consume while working. When comparing these salaries to other workers at the time, the fire chief and police chief of the city were making about $3,600 per year. A fireman made $1.00 per day working a twenty-four hour shift.

John G. Broxterman

John G. Broxterman was Price Hill's own brewmeister, as president of Foss-Schneider Brewing Company. We know from a publication about the development of Glenway-Elberon Heights entitled *Beauty Spots* that he lived at 4714 Glenway Avenue in 1912. John's son, Fred Broxterman, was also in the brewing business as a master brewer. Fred lived on Purcell Avenue in 1910 and Sunset Avenue in 1920.

Beer drinking was encouraged as a part of employment. Thus, most breweries had taprooms. One would find the workers with their big copper mugs taking full advantage of these taprooms. It was not uncommon for others to visit the taproom. What better way to sample the product than right out of the kettle at the proper drinking temperature!

Many funny stories came from tales around the taproom. Police officers and firemen especially liked to stop by the taproom and have a cold one while they were on duty. I was told a story about a hot July day when seven firemen and nine police officers were enjoying a beer at the taproom of a brewery on West Sixth Street. The mayor, on his way home from his office in City Hall, thought he would also stop in for a refreshing brew. On entering the taproom, he encountered the corps of the city's finest. He did not hesitate to sit down

The mug of master brewer Fred Broxterman, son of John G. Broxterman

beside them to enjoy his beer, while asking how all their families were doing. Is it any wonder that over the years, police and firemen referred to Mayor Waldvogel as "Uncle Eddie"?

The taprooms in breweries grew in popularity. They were no longer relegated to a little area next to the boiler rooms, with a place to draw a beer and a tub to wash a glass. They grew into elegant rooms with fine furniture and many sports pictures on the walls. Some were even located on the roofs of breweries, with a

view of the city. The brewery would allow select customers to use these rooms for various occasions, such as retirement parties, even furnishing food. One such brewery taproom was called the Bierstube at Hudepohl Brewery on West Sixth Street.

R. Kleinhans Ice Wagon

Of course, if you couldn't get to the brewery to enjoy your beer, you had to hope there was ice to keep it cold when it got to your local saloon. In Price Hill, some of the most famous ice dealers were R. Kleinhans Ice Dealer, Rumpke, and Gus Wagner, who later opened his own saloon. In later years, Mickey Brogan, who worked for City Ice and Fuel, had an icehouse on Enright Avenue. Mickey knew every saloonkeeper on the Hill. In those days it was not only necessary to keep the beer cold in the ice box, but you had to make sure it was also kept cold until it entered the glass. Thus, the coil box that the beer flowed through had to be iced as well. On any given Sunday a saloonkeeper, suddenly finding his ice supply low, knew that a quick call to Mickey would get him a supply in a hurry.

SINCE 1856

Brucks
Jubilee
BEER

BRUCK'S ALLOWED ONLY 15 MINUTES OF FREE BEER IN THEIR TAP ROOM

"BIG MATE" SET A WORLD RECORD EVERY DAY FOR FAST DRINKING. . .

When Prohibition went into effect, many breweries faced the prospect of going out of business and losing their customers. "Near beer," with less than 1% alcohol content, was permitted under the Volstead Act, so several breweries attempted to fill the demand with this substitute, but it did not prove to be too popular with German beer drinkers. The Bruckman Brewery did produce near beer that tasted good to some drinkers, but most of the breweries quit producing and just closed. When Prohibition ended, Bruckman was the first brewery to produce beer on a large scale again.

Hudepohl Brewery, West End Plant

For a saloon in Price Hill not to have Hudepohl Beer on tap was very unusual. In fact, some saloons only had one beer on tap and that being Hudepohl. Over the years after prohibition, they became one of the largest breweries in the country. In 1948, they produced more than 900,000 barrels of beer.

It is sad when one drives toward Price Hill on the Sixth Street Expressway and sees the dilapidated Hudepohl brewery building, which at one time meant so much to the economy of our city, not to mention how much it meant to the saloons of Price Hill.

LAST CALL

Many of us have lingered in a saloon until way too late, late enough to hear the bartender say, "Last call!" You would hurry up and order that last drink before heading home, while the bartender was trying to protect himself from the law by not serving past the restricted time. One can only imagine what this must have meant on the night of October 27, 1919, in Price Hill and across America. The Volstead Act was to take affect the next day, forbidding the sale of alcoholic beverages.

After four attempts, the likes of Carrie Amelia Moore Nation (known as Carrie Nation) and her friends in both the Daughters of Temperance and the Sons of Temperance organizations, secured a ballot issue that led to a Constitutional amendment outlawing the sale of alcohol in the United States.

It should be noted that from the mid-1800s until 1919, they had tried four times to have the issue passed. On each try it was defeated because of Ohio. The saying that became popular was "As goes Ohio, so goes the nation." It was also added that "As goes Hamilton County, so goes Ohio." On several occasions, the vote in favor of her proposed ban was leading by wide margins, only to have the vote from Hamilton County come in and completely reverse the trend.

One can only imagine what the coming of the Volstead Act meant to the economy of the country. Many establishments selling alcohol were "mom and pop" saloons. Dad was the bartender and mom did the cooking in the kitchen to serve the meals that were usually put out in the saloon. Many other relatives often helped out, too. And the poor doughboys, the servicemen who had only recently returned from fighting in World War I, came home looking to do a little celebrating and found they couldn't even raise a beer to their successes.

Over all, when the dust finally settled some fourteen years later, it proved that the Volstead Act and the 18th Amendment had not curbed the intake of alcoholic beverages in America. Instead, Prohibition was responsible for causing a lot of good honest citizens to go underground and break the law just to secure a drink. Many people were murdered, and politicians, even to the highest level, became corrupt. There are many stories written about major bootleggers like Price Hill's own George Remus, but we hear few stories about the honest small businessman who had his saloon closed and had to try and feed his family by some other means.

Many went underground and tried to keep supplying the drinks people desired. The basements of some of these saloon-keepers suddenly changed to elaborate rathskellers, with nice bars and tables; some even added pinball machines, which later came to be a mainstay in many saloons. One changed his saloon operation to an ice cream parlor, and another converted to a barber shop.

Many small-time bootleggers suddenly appeared to continue to supply those wanting alcohol. Some of them were ready to be up and running again as legal establishments as soon as Prohibition ended. One was "Mary's House," which was at the corner of Bassett Road and Elberon Avenue. As kids we all thought it was just a normal house. Then suddenly a sign appeared over the front door advertising that they sold beer and whiskey.

Mary's did not last too long, though. When Mr. Jasper opened the Mt. Echo Tavern, several doors away, Mary packed up her sign and moved to West Eighth Street and McPherson Avenue, where her place became the "Tip Toe Inn." As kids we used to like to say, "Tip toe in and stagger out!"

I had an uncle who was one of those small-time bootleggers, and he would make his rounds to deliver to his customers. At that time, my family did not have an automobile. Every Sunday he would call up to say he was going to take us for a ride. My dad worked on the railroad and was usually out of town on Sundays. Our uncle would show up, and mom would have my sister and I all dressed. Away we all went in his big Buick. Our first stop was a farm on Queen City Avenue. We would pull up to the barn and my uncle would open the trunk. Men would come out of the barn and load boxes in the trunk. Away we would go, with my sister in the back. I was only three or four years old, sitting in my mother's lap in the front seat. By all appearances, we were just a nice family out for a Sunday drive.

My uncle made many stops at different houses. At each house he would go to the trunk, get out a box, and carry it in the house. The next morning when my dad would come home, he would ask my mom what we did on Sunday. She would tell him about my nice uncle taking us for a ride. My dad, knowing his brother-in-law was a bootlegger, would be furious. Dad knew he was delivering his whiskey. I can remember him saying, "He's going to get all of you killed." I thought maybe he thought my uncle was going to have a wreck or something.

It was not until seven or eight years later that some of my friends asked me to go swimming at this place on Queen City

George Remus (seated) and friends

that only charged you a quarter. It was a lot cheaper than going to Philipps' Swimming Pool. We rode our bikes over, and as I went up the drive and saw a barn, I thought this place looked familiar. I remembered being here when I was a little kid. In later years, as I read about "Death Valley," I thought it was no wonder my dad was so furious and said we were going to get killed. I am sure glad my uncle did not pick one of those Sundays when the federal agents raided George Remus' distributing place. The Death Valley Ranch, located at 2556 Queen City Avenue, was one of George Remus' most fortified distilleries.

Death Valley, George Remus' "farm"

Tales like this are numerous. My wife used to tell us that her father operated what was called a "blind pig" in the Findlay Market area. (A blind pig referred to an establishment that illegally sold alcoholic beverages during Prohibition. An operator would have to disguise his business by charging customers to see an attraction such as a pig, and a complimentary drink was then served.) My wife's family lived upstairs and her father would hide the money in the post of her brass bed. Many a time the police came in and searched all through the house for the money, but they never could find it. As I said before, all Prohibition accomplished was to make a lot of people who were once always honest become dishonest to survive.

GOOD'S

Cafe and Bowling Alley

Wines and Liquors for Medicinal Use.

3210 Warsaw Ave., Price Hill

Alcohol could still be produced for medicinal purposes during Prohibition. That is why big operators tried to buy up wholesale drug houses. On a smaller scale, sometimes if you had a friend who was a druggist, you were able to get a little alcohol from him. I think the funniest thing was the one saloon directly across from the District Three police station advertising "Wines and Liquors for Medicinal Purposes." One has to wonder how many police officers stopped by to cure a bad cold.

Too bad all of us were not of drinking age when Prohibition ended. Looking over all the advertisements from saloons as they got back to business as usual, many advertised a glass of ice cold Hudepohl for only five cents, or maybe you could enjoy a fried spring chicken dinner for only thirty-five cents. You and your best girl could go out with a few bucks in your pocket and really come home loaded.

HOME BREW

During Prohibition, with the saloons all closed, there was no way you were going to keep the Germans of Cincinnati from their beer. Many had honed their skills on making beer either in the old country or by working in the breweries. Thus, the basements of many homes became the places to brew their beer. Mom's copper tub, in which she used to boil clothes, was now pressed into service by the man of the house to boil the hops and malt. Suddenly groceries throughout the area started to display cans of Red Top Malt on their shelves, which was an important part of the brewing process. Some Sunday mornings, walking on the streets where many Germans lived, one would think they were walking amongst the breweries in Cincinnati's Over the Rhine area. (In 1880, Cincinnati was recognized as the "Beer Capital of the World!")

In our house, my father did not drink. Therefore the brewing became the responsibility of my Irish grandmother, who liked

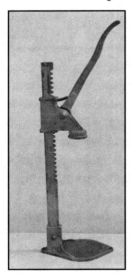

her suds. When I would see her arrive with all the ingredients to brew another batch, I always looked to see if she was carrying a little bottle of root beer extract. You see, it just was not right for the seniors to have their beer and us kids not to have our root beer. The root beer they made for us just could not be reproduced by any soft drink company today.

The job of the youngsters in the home was to put the caps on the bottles after they were filled with beer. We used a capping device that involved placing a silver cap on the bottle, then you used the machine to press down just hard enough to secure the cap — not too hard, or you could break the bottle.

Sometimes we would be lying in bed at night and we would hear what would

A bottle capper in the Price Hill Historical Society Museum

40

sound like an explosion in the basement. "Uh, oh! There goes one of grandma's bottles of beer." You see, after brewing the mix, you then had to move it to a brown crock where it fermented. If one rushed the process and bottled too soon, the gas would build up in the bottle and cause it to explode.

I can remember my two uncles, my grandmother's sons, coming over to sample her latest batch. As they would sit there drinking their beer, they would kid her by telling her it wasn't Guinness, but it sure was good.

She also tried her hand at making wine, but this was reserved mostly for the Christmas holidays. The real

Carrie Nation

winemaking was left to the Italian family that lived across the street. I can remember a truck pulling up in front of their house and unloading box after box of grapes. Then when you went to their basement, the wine barrels lined the walls. It was like going into Meier's Wine Cellar in Silverton. One wonders how they ever drank all that wine. But you soon found out when they had a wedding. It became like the Bible story, everyone with a glass of wine in their hand. Yes, Carrie Nation and her Temperance movement friends may have shut down the saloons, but there was no way was she going to keep a bunch of Germans, Irishmen, and Italians from having a little to drink in Price Hill.

HAPPY DAYS ALONG WARSAW AVENUE

Yes, Prohibition had finally come to an end, and as the popular song of the day said, "Happy Days Are Here Again." Most saloons that had been closed for fourteen long years were eager to get back in business, along with all those businesses that supplied these saloons. From research, it is difficult to find just which saloons in Price Hill were the first to open after Prohibition. One thing that is clear from some of the advertisements of the day, offering nickel beers and cheap meals, is that the reopened saloons were interested in getting back their former customers, plus a lot of new customers. Many of these were veterans who had come home from the World War I (of course, they didn't know it was only the first world war then) and found their favorite watering holes had been shut down. A lot of these bars were along Warsaw Avenue. Our post-Prohibition bar-hopping begins at Warsaw and Hawthorne Avenues, hoping that we will not be too inebriated when we reached St. Lawrence Corner.

Charlie was a bartender at the Fire Hat Tavern on Harrison Avenue in Fairmount. He later became a firefighter, but he was interested in getting back to work as a bartender as soon as he could. The Volstead Act was rescinded on December 5, 1933, and it was time for the bars to begin reapplying for liquor licenses and to get back to work. However, it wasn't that simple. There were a lot of restrictions involved. No Sunday liquor sales were allowed, closing times were specified, and there was even a requirement that all saloons had to sell food. Some got around this by having a bowl of hard boiled eggs on the bar. In Indiana, there was even a restriction that one had to be seated while having a drink, and customers were not permitted to carry a drink from the bar to a table — drinks had to be carried by a waitress. Many of these restrictions still remain as law today, but few are enforced.

The first stop on our bar tour will be at the Trianon Tavern, located at 3110–12 Warsaw Avenue. Mr. Joe Dugan, seeing a need for a nice bar for the enjoyment of both ladies and gentlemen, opened his tavern in November 1946. The Price Hill Civic Club held their meeting at the tavern in April 1947, according to historical records. In the minutes of that meeting, the directors said, "Our hats are off to Mr. Dugan for the up-to-the-minute modern tavern, for location and atmosphere. It is our civic duty to patronize such a fine location."

TRIANON
COCKTAIL LOUNGE
Good Food — Fine Whiskey
Open 'til 2:30 A. M.
3110 WARSAW AVE.   WAbash 9704

The Trianon rated second to none for food and beverages — it was a friendly place with friendly prices. And Mr. Dugan always said, "If you get a headache here, go across the street and see my brother Bill. He'll take care of it." You see, his brother Bill operated a drug store right across Warsaw Avenue for years.

Mr. Joe Dugan operated the tavern for about eight years, and when he decided to retire, he sold the business to the Brannigans. Mr. Brannigan, along with his sons Don and Roger, operated the business in the same manner for more than forty years.

Next along Warsaw Avenue was a place called the Eureka Bar at 3116 Warsaw Avenue. It's not clear as to the exact date it opened, but we know from Mr. Kline's daughter, Phyllis Kline, that it was up and running in 1935, and when he ran it, the place was called Kline's Café. It was next to the firehouse at the corner of Warsaw and Considine, and when the great Ohio River flood of 1937 hit, Kline's was delegated the task of distributing clean drinking water. Having no beer to dispense anyway, Mr. Kline was happy to take on the task of water distribution. Phyllis thinks the fire department delegated the job to the café next door so they could concentrate on firefighting. There were long lines of people with containers for water lined up all day long. One has to remember that the water works had shut down because of the flood. Just think, the '37 flood was the only time I can re-

43

member getting off school, as we had no such thing as snow days in those years.

Around 1938, Phyllis' father sold the business to a Mr. Francisco and went to work at the Palace Café/Paradise Gardens on Sixth Street downtown. Mr. Francisco, who renamed the place the Eureka Bar, was also operating a pet shop next door at the same time. What a funny situation, but I guess he thought it would not be too difficult dealing with a different kind of animal when they had a little too much to drink.

Mr. Francisco really made a change in the place by forming a social club. This was quite different than many social clubs on the Hill. As one can see by the advertisement, "Membership can be obtained on applications at the Eureka Bar." With most social clubs, one just walked in the door and you were a member.

I guess Mr. Francisco must have gone back to tending his pets, because after awhile he sold out to the Brannigans. Maybe they wished to maintain the dignity and the good name built up at the Trianon over the years, as the Eureka was referred to as the "Red Neck Bar." No, it did not change names, that was just an indication of who was hanging out there. One thing we know for sure is that Mutt Connelly, the "walking bookie" on Warsaw Avenue, was allowed to talk to customers in the Eureka Bar but not the Trianon. The Brannigans were trying to maintain the Trianon as a high-class saloon.

It must be mentioned that Mr. Brannigan passed on and his son, Don, took over the ownership. By this time, his brother Roger was operating his own establishment, known as Wolfer's Tavern, on Glenway Avenue opposite Fairbanks Avenue. Over the years, this had been a neighborhood bar competing with Coney's Bar. Maybe one could say that all those that Mr. Coney had run out had made their way several blocks down the street.

Now back to the Trianon and Eureka with Don Brannigan at the helm. He had a liking for police officers. On any given morning shortly past 7:00 am, it was hard to distinguish whether there were more police at District 3's lineup or those going off-duty and standing at the bar at the Trianon.

It is worth mentioning that a firefighter came along and didn't like all these policemen hanging out in a bar three doors away from the old firehouse. So he up and bought the place and named it the Firehouse Sports Bar. He should have known that sports bars at the time did not go over too well in Price Hill. By the late 1970s, both the Trianon and the Eureka were no more.

We will now make our way across Warsaw Avenue to a saloon that has connections clear to Hollywood. Yes, Welz Tavern at 3113 Warsaw Avenue was owned by Doris Day's Uncle Charlie. In fact, she got her start in singing by practicing in the apartment on the second floor, where she lived along with her mother and aunt. At this time she was not singing professionally, but practicing to sing in an amateur contest at the Little Club at the

3113 Warsaw Avenue, the location of Welz Tavern

old Lookout House in Kentucky. As a youngster, I remember my friends and I sat in a booth at the tavern and she served us. Her aunt made some of the best barbecue sandwiches in town, and they only cost fifteen cents.

The years passed, and Doris changed her name from Kappelhoff to Day and made her way into Hollywood. Her uncle and aunt got out of the saloon business. Many more owners with different names took over until it finally took the name of Dittleberger's Brau Haus. Today it is closed.

STAR'S FORMER HOME
HAS SEEN BETTER DAYS

Nancy Dittleberger has heard the stories about Doris Kappelhoff sitting in Charley Welz's tavern on Warsaw Avenue in East Price Hill, singing along with the juke-box or the radio.

Years later, Doris Kappeloff would win fame in Hollywood under the name of Doris Day. But she began her singing career while living in an apartment above the tavern.

The old tavern, owned by Day's uncle, Charlie, has gone through changes over the years and now is Dittelberger's Brau Haus, in the 3100 block of Warsaw Avenue, an area that community activists and business owners are trying to rejuvenate.

"It was a typical Cincinnati tavern, with beef barbecue and hot potato salad, homemade chili and fabulous beer," Dittleberger said of the tavern in the 1970 book, *Doris Day, Her Own Story*, by A. E. Hotchner.

From the Cincinnati Enquirer, by Mike Turmell, published February 18, 1991. Reprinted with permission.

A few doors up Warsaw Avenue and across Considine Avenue is our next saloon. The Good Café and Bowling Alleys at 3210 Warsaw, previously just the Good Café, sold "Wine and Liquor for Medicinal Purposes" legally under the Volstead Act.

Now, with the end of Prohibition, Ed Good could go back to his real job of operating a bowling alley (not much of one with only six lanes) and selling real alcohol. In 1946, Good decided to retire and George Hock, who operated the saloon "Opposite the Incline," decided to make the move to Warsaw Avenue. It was a smart move, since the Incline wasn't operating anymore. Business was getting pretty bad, but they did have the best bean soup. And at ten cents a bowl, you couldn't beat the price. I knew Mrs. Lane, who served as a waitress for many years. She loved to see us big spenders come in for a bowl of soup and a Coke. If she got a dime tip out of anyone of us, she really felt good.

It is interesting to note that when George Hock made the move to the bright lights of Warsaw Avenue, he really spiced up the menu. He added oysters, shrimp, steak, and the like to the fare he served; he even put Michelob on tap. The trouble was that George and his sons did not stick around too long. In July 1951 they decided, after making all that money with high-class beer, that they were going to retire. Along came a couple of former firemen who had been running a saloon at West Eighth Street and State Avenue. Frank Sefton and Ray Suttendorf decided to try their luck in the bright lights. After about five years they found out that they could make more money in furnished rooms, so they gave up the saloon business, too.

The new owners decided the place needed a new name, so they changed the name to Warsaw Bar. With all the bars on Warsaw Avenue it was good to see one that bore the name of the street. They served three pieces of chicken, a roll, and cole slaw for a buck, which in today's world could have run KFC out of business. By the same token, around this time the bigger

OYSTERS
RAW - FRIED - STEWED
SHRIMP - FISH - STEAKS
Home Cooked Plate Lunches Served Daily
Michelob Beer On Tap
OPEN BOWLING SATURDAY AND SUNDAY
PLATE LUNCHES Served from 10a.m. Till 6p.m.
HOCK CAFE
3208-10 Warsaw Avenue   Wabash 9766

bowling alleys with 36 and 48 lanes ran these guys out of the bowling business; they now concentrated on food and drinks. After about six years, with so many saloons in the neighborhood, they went totally out of business and the East Price Hill Improvement Association bought the building.

Ollie's Café was located at 3222 Warsaw Avenue, at the corner of Purcell Avenue. He had Royal Amber on tap. In those days that was the "cream of the crop." I would bet he also had Hudepohl on tap. Ollie was good about sponsoring softball and Knothole teams. In those days, to sponsor a Knothole team cost about ten bucks for shirts, five for caps, and a few dollars more for a couple of bats and balls. You could get by for less than twenty-five bucks, but to a saloonkeeper, that might have been their twenty-five bucks profit from a day's work. Of course, in those days, there was no writing it off on their income tax, either.

I always liked Ollie. You see, I used to collect for the *Enquirer* for Pete Massari, owner of the paper route, when I was about 10 years old. Whenever I went by Ollie's, the bill would be 45 cents, he would give me a half buck and say keep the change. A nickel tip was a lot when you only got a quarter to do collecting for a couple of hours. I would take that nickel and run up the street to Strassburger's Bakery and tell Ida to give me two jelly donuts. I always made sure to get Ida to wait on me because she always threw in a cream roll. Imagine all that for a nickel today; it would probably set you back more than two bucks.

Woodlawn Hall

The Woodlawn Bowling Lanes and Hall were upstairs on Warsaw Avenue at Woodlawn. After running the saloon at Price Avenue near Hawthorne for many years, Gus Wagner decided to move onto bigger things. He opened at this location some of the finest bowling lanes in the city, with many top bowlers bowling in various leagues. The upstairs hall was the scene of many wedding receptions. On Saturday nights, various clubs from the Hill would also rent the hall and have their dances and drinks here. One thing for sure, they had the steepest set of steps leading to the second floor. If you were not sober, you better have someone help you down or you would end up in the middle of Warsaw Avenue.

In those days, it was important to be a union bar, even if you only had a couple of employees. Staunch union members would refuse to go in any bar that did not display the union sign.

Sadly, Gus got sick and passed on. After that, several other owners operated the bar over the years, and finally the bowling alleys were removed. The downstairs became the Chatterbox Dance Hall. With all the fights that occurred there, a better name would have been "The Punch Bowl." Thanks to the neighbors, the city refused to renew their license and the Chatterbox and Woodlawn Hall became just a memory.

Few are around who will remember the next saloon on our tour. When we think of the Knights of Columbus on Price Hill, we think of the Mother Seton Council, which called the old Sunset Theater at Glenway and Sunset Avenues their home for many years. But long before they came into being, there was a Price Hill Knights of Columbus. Some of the most prominent Catholic men on the Hill were members, and in the early 1900s they had their home at the corner of Warsaw and Fairbanks Avenues. It was reported to be one of the finest halls in the state of Ohio. At the

Price Hill Knights of Columbus Hall

time, if one wanted to have any kind of special function in Price Hill, this was the place to have it. Like all other establishments serving alcohol, it had suffered during Prohibition, however. But with the repeal of Prohibition, not only did the hall reopen, they also added a garden, along with music and dancing. I guess as one looks at all the German names in the roster for the Knights of Columbus, you'd figure they also did a lot of beer drinking. But soon the Depression was in full swing and no one was spending much money. Not only did the Price Hill Knights of Columbus go out of business, but they went bankrupt and all the property went into the courts. For many years the property sat vacant until the late 1940s, when the Price Hill Roller Rink was built on the site. Many guys from all over the Hill enjoyed skating there with their favorite girlfriends.

Just a few doors up the street at 3509 Warsaw Avenue, Red Richmond operated Price Hill Recreation. It was a super bowling alley, along with a bar and restaurant. Many a youngster got their first job setting up pins at the bowling alley. One really had to work in those days. With no automatic pin setters, all the work was done by hand. You pressed a little pedal with your foot and little spikes came up on the alley and you placed a pin on each of the spikes. You had to do all of that for a nickel a line. For five

51

bowlers, you got a quarter, and for three games, you made 75 cents for the night. Of course if you were really good, you could jump alleys and double your night's wages. But remember, you also had to get your homework done, so you couldn't stay out too late.

Red was a real nice guy, always good to kids. He weighed about four hundred and fifty pounds, and when you saw his car coming down the street, if it leaned to one side, you knew Red was driving. In later years, his son Jack took over the business, but the new super bowling alleys made it difficult for the smaller places to compete. Finally Jack gave up the bowling business and, for awhile, operated a saloon at Western Hills Shopping Center.

As mentioned earlier, Joe Brauer operated the saloon at Warsaw and McPherson Avenues for years. As he got older, it was time to retire and it then became Witte Tavern. To follow an act like Joe was very hard. After Witte closed the saloon, it became Scheve Hardware. It is a testimony as to how buildings were built in those days. The building still serves as a hardware store and, from the looks of this building, it may well last another hundred years.

WITTE TAVERN

Formerly Ben Brauer

Billiard Room   *Ladies Invited*

●

3515 WARSAW AVE.   WAbash 9555

BROTHER, CAN YOU LOAN ME A NICKEL?

That might be what customers at Jos. Brauer's bar at McPherson and Warsaw Avenues asked when they were low on cash. Not only could a person enjoy a glass of beer but maybe could apply for a loan because the place also was the home of the Price Hill Electric Savings & Loan Association, the forerunner to today's United Savings Association. The Brauers founded the company and stashed all the records in an attic.

From "The Hill," May 10, 1977. Reprinted with permission of the Price Hill Press.

If you were getting a little hungry, you had to stop at Stone's Chili Parlor and have a bowl of chili. It was much different from the chili we know today. Mother Stone's chili was more like the chili we used to get at home on a Saturday night. It was heavy on tomatoes, with a can of kidney beans thrown in, and light on the hot spices. I think Stone's made more on their pinball machine than the chili, though. With only four stools and two tables, the crowd came and went in a hurry.

Our next stop would be the Club Embassy at 3602 Warsaw Avenue, one door east of McPherson Avenue. Our host here was Danny Coletta. To prove he was Italian, he made some of the best ravioli you'd ever taste. His patrons always looked for-

54

ward to the Sunday before Christmas. He would have a big open house with plenty of his great ravioli, plus lots of spaghetti and meatballs, and everything was on the house.

In later years, after Danny Coletta left, a younger crowd moved in. Suddenly one of these youngsters noted how high the bar was from the floor — in fact, it was the highest bar in town. So they began making bets to see who could jump straight up and land on the bar. This activity made for a lot of bruised shins, and this might be where the real bar-hopping began.

Maybe someone should have named the Old Timer's Bar at 3531 Warsaw Avenue the "Good Times Bar." Over the years they were always having a good time, be it a picnic, a ballgame, or the like. Their distribution of Christmas baskets to the needy of Price Hill was a tradition for many years.

It seems that Charlie Schoch, the owner of the Old Timer's Bar for years, was a part of every club on the Hill. In one of his ads he advertised a gallon jug of beer for eighty cents. In days past it was popular for saloonkeepers, on their off day, to visit other establishments, sort of like a busman's holiday. Mom Poli, who operated a saloon in Riverside, stopped by to pay a visit to Charlie. It was on a Friday night, but Charlie wasn't there. Mom, having a good voice, took to the piano and belted out a few tunes, to the delight of the patrons there that night. They were glad Charlie was not there, because she promised to do an encore when Charlie was there. People were glad to know in advance because they knew that Mom Poli would pack the place for her second show. Is there any wonder why many said this should be the Good Times saloon?

Martin's Tavern at 3542 Warsaw Avenue was owned by Ed and Tom Martin. As they say, "It was a friendly meeting place." Both of the owners were raised in Price Hill and had many friends who stopped by. They sponsored several softball teams throughout the Hill. This was a family café where you could bring your kids along to have a Coke while you enjoyed a beer, being assured that foul language would not be allowed. After awhile the saloon business got to them, though. Tom enjoyed retirement, while Ed went on to being a good salesman for Glenway Chevrolet.

For years you could not miss Frank's Bar at 3617 Warsaw Avenue as you exited from the Kroger parking lot. Frank's was on one side of the driveway and Huber's Dry Good Store was on the other side. Over the years it went from a nice bar to what I've already referred to as a "punch bowl," a place more known for the fights than the fun. In the summer of 1966, a lady came out of the bar and shot her husband in the parking lot; from this time on things went downhill. I think the owner was glad that

---

MARTIN'S TAVERN
A FRIENDLY PLACE TO MEET

GOOD FOOD
WINE - BEER

OPEN 'TIL 1 A. M.

●

3542 WARSAW AVE.   Wabash 9808

Kroger decided to enlarge their parking lot and offered to buy his property.

Fred Wessels owned the Bohemian Grill at 3656 Warsaw Avenue. For awhile it became quite confusing to some people if you said, "I will meet you at the Bohemian," because there were two Bohemians on the Hill; more on the other one later. This saloon was just a few doors from St. Lawrence Church. A lot of men who attended Mass at the church went from benediction to having a little good cheer at the Bohemian Grill.

Mr. Wessels' son Bill (who later became a firefighter), along with a group of his buddies from around the St. Lawrence Corner area, formed what became known as the "Aces Club." Bill said they formed under a street light at the corner of McPherson Avenue and VanVey Street, and this is where they held their meetings until they came of drinking age. They then made the rear room of the Bohemian their place to meet. Being so close to St. Lawrence, if one became a little too boisterous, the bartender would give them a friendly reminder that they were next to the church. After Mr. Wessels passed on, the saloon changed hands several times and finally it was torn down and became a parking lot for the church.

WILLIAM WESSELS, 76, WAS
FIREFIGHTER FOR 30 YEARS

Retired Cincinnati firefighter William Wessels . . . died March 21, 2003 . . . attended St. Lawrence School and graduated from Edler High School in 1945. His parents operated the old Bohemian Grill on Warsaw Avenue in Price Hill.

. . .

In 1949, he joined the Cincinnati Fire Department and worked for Engine Company 45, which was at Court and Plum and later moved to its current locaiton at 5th and Central Avenues. He was an engineer and operated the pumper. . . . In his early years, he enjoyed playing first base for the Fire Department's slow-pitch softball team.

He retired in 1979 and enjoyed golfing as well as woodworking. He had kept in touch with a group of friends from grade school who called themselves the Aces Club. The boys would meet at the corner of Van Vey and McPherson Streets in Price Hill.

Just before his death, Mr. Wessels began writing a history of the Aces Club. "We would meet and solve world problems, play cards, etc. Fines were ordered for being late, vulgarity, missing books, or just missing." Sixty-two years later, the club still operates under those same rules. . . .

From an obituary written by Karen Andrew in the Cincinnati Enquirer, March 2003. Reprinted with permission.

I guess there were so many saloons that we just ran out of names for them on the Hill. Perhaps that's why the owner of the 51 Bar at 3751 Warsaw Avenue took the last two numbers in the address. Some also have said that this was the fifty-first liquor license to be issued in Price Hill, and that's how it got its number name. It could have been that they took the name from a very popular bar in downtown Cincinnati at that time, known as the "51 Bar." Some real characters hung around here and, sad to say, many of them were firefighters. The bar moved on to better things on Glenway Avenue and took its name with it; more on this later.

THE BARSTOOLS ON WEST EIGHTH STREET

We have just completed our tour of the saloons on Warsaw, but hold onto your barstool, because our journey has just begun! Our journey continues along West Eighth Street, and the first stop will be at the Sovereign Restaurant in Queen's Tower. Some may say this certainly wasn't a saloon, but they did serve alcohol, some of the best food in town, and an amazing view. One would have to say that the New Price Hill House, which opened in the early 1930s, just came along a little too soon because it lasted only several years.

But as one would sit in the Sovereign looking at the view, it was easy to think back to the Price Hill House advertising a veranda that seated one thousand people. With not many buildings to block the view, I guess one could virtually "see forever." Sitting in the dining room at this location today, your view stretches from Bromley, Kentucky, clear to the water tower in Mount Washington. In the past it was said that few visitors from out of town visited Mr. Price's Buttermilk Hill. Today the Sovereign Restaurant has changed to the Primavista Restaurant. With the great view and the fabulous food, many locals now proudly bring their out-of-town guest here for dinner.

There was a saloon located at the northwest corner of West Eighth Street and Matson Place that was sold by Mr. Hock, who moved on to Warsaw Avenue. The new owners at this West Eighth Street location chose the name of the Wren House Café. Someone said they didn't know where they came up with this name, but, for sure, a bunch of birds hung out here. After World War II, many returning servicemen from the neighborhood frequented the Wren House and formed a club known as "The Hilltoppers." This club put many good softball teams on the field at Dempsey Park. Many of the Hilltoppers found their wives among the sisters of some of the fellows who belonged to the club.

Veering off Eighth Street at the bottom of the hill will take you to Grand Avenue. We sure would not want to miss the Holy Family Gym. With their two bowling alleys, they are probably the oldest continuous bowling establishment in the state of Ohio. Sometimes I have to laugh when I think how strict the State Liquor Board is about the distance a saloon has to be from a school. Here we have one right under the classrooms. How well I can remember the good nun leading us out to recess in the second grade. We had to go right down the steps and past the bar. I would guess because over all these years it operated as a private club, they were exempt from the law.

The Holy Family Gym Bar has operated for more than 90 years, and in all that time it has only had four different bartenders. A long list of clubs called the gym their home, beginning with the Celtics, Flat Feet, Kitty Klub, Delta Chi, Troubadours, etc. I am sure I have missed quite a few. Also, many good basketball games took place in the gymnasium. Then, going back to the 1930s, many good boxing matches were put on in the gym. Here the likes of Ezzard Charles and Jack Marmer took to the ring. (Jack Marmer also operated shoe stores in Price Hill for many years.)

We stopped by Mr. Mause's saloon earlier in this book, but the saloon at West Eighth Street and Enright Avenue has a lot more life to it. During Prohibition, Mr. Mause went out of the saloon business. Mr. Krieger took over after Prohibition, renaming the saloon the Wm. Krieger Café. It became a popular stop for many of the older generation, especially with the rear room which was advertised as the "Ladies' Sitting Room." Also the garden was opened and was popular in the summer, since no air conditioning existed at that time. With only a few small fans to blow the air around, things could get pretty hot in a saloon on a summer day. Mr. Krieger operated the saloon for a good number of years and then the new owner renamed it "Bob's Den."

BAR TO REOPEN HISTORIC BEER GARDEN

The new owner of the Lyon's Den Café on West Eighth Street is restoring a tradition at his "family" bar.

Bill Richter of Delhi, who recently bought the bar, is spending $3,000 to repair the beer garden. He said it hasn't been used for almost 10 years.

Before it fell into disuse, he said, the beer garden was a hub of activity for more than 100 years.

"I remember the good times I had (in the garden)," Richter said, explaining why he decided to restore it.

He said he expects to attract groups ranging from friends and families to athletic teams to the garden.

From Price Hill Press, June 20, 1990. Reprinted by permission.

WM. KRIEGER'S CAFE
West Eighth and Enright

Bob's Den operated under this name until around 1956 when along came Jimmy and Velma Lyons. For ten years prior they had operated Carley's and had gone into retirement for a year or so. Jim did not like playing golf and got tired of sitting around the house, so he decided to do what he knew best and got back in the saloon business. The name "Bob" didn't look good, so he renamed the place "The Lyon's Den Café."

Recently, one of our Price Hill Historical Society volunteers, Joyce Meyer, went to lunch at the historic Market Street Grill in Harrison, Ohio. Ironically, as I was writing this book, she found a connection there to Price Hill. The lunch menu includes the history of their restaurant, built around 1850. It is described in detail and includes all the renovations and additions to the building. The following caption is directly from that menu: "In the main dining room one can find an old back bar that was originally located in a Price Hill bar called the Lyons Den. We stripped and stained the back bar to bring it back to life."

Joyce was able to speak to one of the owners of the Market Street Grill, who told her how they acquired the bar. During the renovation of the bar area in the restaurant, an inspector told one of the owners that he had an old bar. It was located in the basement of his Delhi home. The owners went to see the bar, purchased and reinstalled it in their establishment. Today it enhances the historic Market Street Grill.

The Lyon's Den was quite a change for Jim and Velma. At Carley's they always had a young crowd with a full house over the weekends. They now had a saloon inhabited by a much older neighborhood crowd.

About fourteen years later, they decided to retire for good and sold the bar to Bill Richter. Bill rehabbed the old outdoor garden by adding a few horseshoe pits and brought in a younger

The old Lyon's Den back bar, now at at the Market Street Grill

bunch of patrons, especially a lot of softball players after their nightly games.

Over the next few years several other owners tried their hands at being barkeepers and in early 2009 the place was closed and boarded up. Everyone suspected that this was the last hurrah of the famous saloon. Then suddenly new life started to spring up and a sign with palm trees announced the opening of "Paradise Lounge." We wonder how Mr. Mause would take to the palm trees! For sure he and all his neighbors, who now lie in the cemetery across the street, are happy that they won't have to go far for a drink if they ever come back to life. I guess many would say, "From one paradise to another!"

I will briefly mention the Tip Toe Inn located at the corner of West Eighth Street and McPherson Avenue. I only visited this saloon twice in my life. I should not have gone back the second time. Not that there was anything wrong with the saloon, but a professional barfly hung out here. Not only did he get me once, but he got me twice. As the old saying goes, "Sucker once, shame on him, sucker twice, shame on you." This guy was an old firefighter and, as you walked into the bar, he gave you a big hello and would say, "Have a beer on me." By this time, the bartender was drawing up two beers. You would drink up and, of course, you couldn't leave without buying him one back. So you would say, "Give my buddy a drink and I will have a beer as well." My buddy would immediately tell the bartender that he will have a double off the top shelf. Suddenly the dime beer he bought cost me a buck and a half for his top shelf double. As I said before, I walked in once more and he got me again. But from that day forward I vowed to never go back to the Tip Toe Inn, even knowing he had passed on several years previously.

The Cottage Tavern was located at 4068 West Eighth Street. Mr. Wellman was the original owner of the tavern. Over the years it has had several different owners, along with several different names. Being close to Saint William Church, it was also known to host a few drinkers after Sunday Mass. Prior to World War II, many young men from the area hung out in this saloon, forming a club known as The Palos Club. They also put some pretty good ballplayers on local fields. Two of these players were the Mercurio brothers, Joe and Tom, who purchased the saloon in 1946.

The brothers named the tavern Mercurio's and introduced Italian food to the menu. They also added music and increased the daytime crowd. After a few years it was time to move on, and the Smiley family took ownership and changed the name to Sunset Lounge. For some reason a bunch of motorcycle people began to hang out there. The neighbors would get quite upset when the motorcycles revved up as they left, sometime after one o'clock in the morning. Calls to the police department became very frequent.

Not liking to deal with the police, the Smiley family sold the tavern to Maury Bibent. He was the son of the owner of a well-known eating place, Maury's Tiny Cove in Cheviot, Ohio. He took over and also had several run-ins with the police. Before long, he went back to Cheviot. Then, along came Pete Witte and his brother, Herb. Pete had acquired the building, which was part of the property adjacent to his engraving business, at the corner of Sunset Avenue and West Eighth Street. The name of the tavern was the changed to "The Kohlhaus." It was in keeping

with the kind of building, which reminded one of a German pub. They introduced German beer and German food, and they set up an outdoor patio space in front of the saloon. Pete soon realized, like most former owners, that the parking situation was not too good at that location. In the front of the saloon, parking was prohibited from 4 to 6 p.m. When the church was having any kind of function, it took away other street parking. He attempted to attract those going and coming from Elder football games and also added entertainment on the weekends. In the end he found out that he was doing much better in the engraving business than the saloon business and sold out. The saloon does continue to operate under new ownership.

Our next stop along the way is at West Eighth Street and Trenton Avenue, the location of the original Trenton Café. Here one

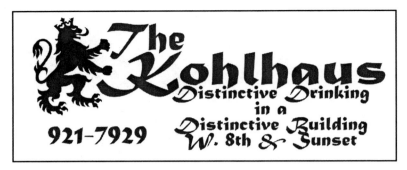
could get a jug of beer for thirty-five cents or a whole keg for $2.25. Of course, this was in 1936. Shortly after that it became Abatico's Restaurant, serving a plate of spaghetti or ravioli for thirty-five cents. Believe me, they had the best ravioli anyone would want to eat. I am sure glad my wife is not here to hear that. She made ravioli and would kill me if I said someone else's was better.

With such a small place and such good food, they needed to move on and expand. They opened the Turf and Field downtown. This was during the war years and their business really took off. After this, Abatico's became known as the C & H Café,

catering to many young servicemen returning from the war who lived in the Trenton Avenue area. One of these happened to be Tubby Thompson, who at the time was working as a sheet metal man. He, along with his wife Dolly, who was a New York native, purchased the saloon and as Tubby always said, "Things are a lot different when you're on the other side of the bar."

Tubby passed on in September of 1991 and Dolly continued to operate the saloon for several years before deciding to sell out. The saloon still operates under the Trenton Tavern name.

The Blue Note, located at the corner of West Eighth Street and Overlook Avenue, opened in the mid-1940s. Norma Berryman was the owner; although small in stature, she did not take any guff from the patrons. Over the years it was always a young adult's bar and the only thing served was beer, most of that was 3.2% draft variety.

On any given Sunday afternoon, when it first opened, it hosted some of the best jazz sessions that anyone would desire.

The Blue Note, West Eighth and Overlook

Usually the place was packed wall to wall from 2 pm in the afternoon until 7 pm at night. The crowd at the Blue Note was a mixture of many veterans returning home to find a lot of graduates there from Elder and Western Hills High schools. Added to this mixture were a lot of young ladies, who had just graduated from Seton or Western Hills and were just entering the working world, looking for a good time on the weekend.

68

NORMA BERRYMAN

Norma Mary Berryman, 84, Price Hill, died Oct. 17 in Mandeville, La. She was the owner of the Blue Note Café. Survivors include her husband Garland Berryman; daughter Brandy Bone; sister Rose Sullivan; grandchildren Chris Chalk, Kerri Profitt, Kasey Rouse, Jenna and Adam Mohl, Kim, Greg, Curt and Jeff Bone; and great-grandchild Daniel Chalk. She was the mother of the late Noreen Ryan and Sherry Ulm.

Services were Oct. 26 at St. Teresa of Avila; burial in St. Mary Cemetery. Arrangements made by B. J. Meyer Sons Funeral Home. Memorials may be made to the Alzheimer's Association.

From the Cincinnati Enquirer, published October 28, 2000. Reprinted with permission.

Things changed somewhat in the late 1950s. As my friend Frank who, by the way, drew most of the cartoons in this book, put it, "One afternoon I saw a good looker go into a lounge called The Blue Note. Found out the good looker's name was Jan and she was a barmaid at the lounge. Jan talked me into coming up some weekend for their sing-a-long. Thus instead of being a solitary drinker, I split my time 50/50, singing and drinking."

It was great fun, but all good things have to come to an end. A new owner came along and out went the piano and in came the pool tables. Yes, this was an era that brought in a whole new clientele. Over the next several years the saloon became a biker bar with lots of trouble for the police and the neighbors. The next thing you knew, the place closed. After being closed for several years, along came a guy by the name of Doug Gundrum. His father wanted him to open a pizza place in Clifton, but he chose to go into the saloon business. After many months of doing most of the rehabbing on his own, he was ready to open. Out with the bikers and in came the young adult crowd again, many were attending college either at Mount Saint Joseph College or the University of Cincinnati. He brought in some of the blues bands that were playing the circuit at the time and packed the house not only on weekends, but throughout the week.

Pretty soon it became time to expand not only the dance area, but also to add a sand volleyball court. Over the years the club became an institution on the Hill as well as in music circles around the city. The crowds were large and with no parking lot, on some nights, parking for many was several blocks away. Again the neighbors became angry. They were angry about the parking and the loud music. But, over the years, Doug worked along with the Civic Club (our community council) to try and keep things in hand.

Many who once frequented the club grew older and now had families. So, the bar circuit was no longer their thing. They decided that the next best thing was to form a club, the Blue Note Social Club. For awhile they met at the bar and then later their meetings became a picnic in the summer and a few other social get-togethers.

In 2008, Doug Gundrum had enough of the bar business and decided to sell out. The bar still operates under the same format. Its name has changed to "Harveys." And if you drive by on a weekend night, you may notice that the crowds are a lot slimmer.

Looking out the front door of the Blue Note and directly across the street, one could see the Curnayn's Tavern. Originally it was known as Monk's Place. In the mid-1950s Curnayn's was the place to go, not only to get your alcoholic beverages but also your meals. Six deluxe hamburgers for a buck; even White Castle couldn't compete at that price. Many Catholics frequented the

---

M O N K ' S   P L A C E
HOME-MADE
CHILI and TURTLE SOUP
The Coldest Beer in Town - Sandwiches of All Kinds
4515 W. EIGHTH   WABASH 9817

tavern and for Lent they even served up a bowl of real turtle soup for a quarter.

Over the years, this bar had a lot of whiskey customers. You know the guy who would show up in the morning before going to work with his hands shaking. He could hardly throw down the double shot without spilling it. After a few beer chasers, he would throw down another and out the door and off to work he would go. You later found out that he was a tool-and-die maker and needed steady hands to do his work. You wondered how he could work at all. But with that little stop in the morning, he was steady as could be for the rest of the day.

In the 1970s, Mr. Yunger bought the café, but the name remained Curnayn's. He, along with his family, had operated a café in Findlay Market for years. Being Hungarian, they put out some of the best food anyone would want to eat. On any given Saturday you had to wait in line to get a table. Many politicians from the Court House frequented the place in Findlay Market. It was only natural that they made their way to the Hill and to Curnayn's bar.

Hendly Brink, who was a bailiff for Judge Nurre, was famous on Election Day. He carried out a tradition started by his father by always cooking up a batch of bean soup along with cottage ham and serving it at the saloon. Almost any politician of the day knew that if they were to get the vote in the 25th Ward, they had better make a visit to Curnayn's and get a bowl of his soup. They also knew it was a good idea to buy a round of drinks. On Saturdays throughout the summer, the place would fill with golfers, who had just finished their rounds at Dunham Golf Course. Thus, a lot of talk went on about why their scores were so high or so low.

The saloon continues to operate under new management. For awhile, a few bad apples made their way in as customers. The police threatened to close them up. Thanks to the owners, they made sure these people were gone and the saloon again operated as it had for years past.

We now will go catty-corner across West Eighth Street to the Jack and Jill Café. I will say this, when Mr. Heffernan had his two daughters behind the bar, they were the prettiest barmaids on the Hill. On any given Friday night, when there was an Elder football game, one could be assured that after the game much discussion went on here as to why the team won or lost.

This was probably one of the first saloons to have horseshoe courts in their rear yard. During the summer, some of the best players in the city showed how the game was played. If you couldn't throw a ringer with each shoe, this was not the place for you. They also had a very active social club. Their elected officers were very active with the money they raised for various events, and did many charitable things throughout the Hill. After Mr. John Heffernan (the owner of Jack and Jill Café) passed on in the 1970s, the place closed. His nephew, Joe, was the manager of the Cuvier Press Club, a popular club for politicians and businessmen in the downtown area.

GOOD COLD BEER	STEAKS and CHOPS
JACK & JILL CAFE	
TWO FINE HORSESHOE COURTS	A UNION HOUSE
You'll Have a Good Time When You Stop Here	EIGHTH and OVERLOOK PRICE HILL

We have covered many saloons along Warsaw Avenue and West Eighth Street. One in today's world might ask how so many saloons could survive by being almost next to one another. Surely there could not have been that many people drinking all the time. But you must remember that many of these saloons operated in a time with no television. In order to watch a ballgame you made your way to the local bar and crowded around a little ten-inch television set behind the bar. That time was quit different from today, where you go into a sports bar and the TVs hit you from every side.

The old saloons had pinball machines and jukeboxes to help pay the rent. (Ray Bigner's Wesco Novelty Co. and Westerhaus Amusement Company were two companies that supplied most of the pinball machines and jukeboxes for Price Hill saloons.) There was nothing worse for a poor bartender than some guy coming in who had just broken up with his girlfriend. He might pop a buck in the jukebox and play some song his girlfriend liked, ten times in a row. After about three rounds, the bartender and the patrons were ready to kill the guy. And we cannot rule out that many of the bars had a "book" either in the back room or a "walking bookie" that made his rounds each day, and the saloonkeeper would get a cut of that business.

GOOD OLD DAYS ON GLENWAY

As we make our way to Glenway Avenue, we will skip over the Ballinasloe Café, Coney's Saloon, and Wolfer's Café, which were all mentioned earlier. Our first stop will be at Shuller's Café located at 3821 Glenway Avenue. This place really threw a curve at me. I was thinking of Shuller's Party Hall located where Hoinke Bowling Alley was. After some research I came to realize that this saloon had to be located in the building where the liquor store was for years. This was yet another bar that opened up shortly after the repeal of Prohibition with a Hudepohl draught beer for five cents a glass. The thing that really caught my eye was that after the fireworks at Mt. Echo Park,

Everyone Says:

"SHULLER'S IS THE NICEST PLACE ON PRICE HILL!"

Hudepohl's Draught Beer
5c a glass

Musical Program Saturday Night from 9:00 till 1 a. m.
After Mt. Echo Celebration July 4th Stop at Shuller's

Lunches

Sandwiches

ICE COLD BOTTLE BEER to take out!

Shuller's Cafe
3821 Glenway Ave.

many people would stop at Shuller's. All I can remember were the fireworks, having lived for years at the base of the park. I imagine there are very few alive today who enjoyed a cold one at Shuller's Café.

Our next stop will be directly across the street at Bahlke's Café located at 3826 Glenway Avenue. Bob Bahlke was the owner. He later sold out to Mr. Boehl who renamed it Boehl's Musical Bar. What a good time one could have in this saloon, especially on a Sunday night. You see, Mr. Boehl had a friend by the name of Kert Aylward who operated a bar on Main Street in Covington, Kentucky. Kert had been in the entertainment field and was a good singer, so on Sunday nights he would have amateur night. Those in attendance could take the mike and belt out a tune.

Since amateur night was so popular at the place across the river, Mr. Boehl gave it a try at his place. The bar had a nice stage behind it, with all glass mirrors, making the place look much bigger than it was. On the stage was a piano that was played during the weekends. Sunday nights were reserved for the amateurs belting out some good tunes, especially the young ladies who would often sing duets. But like every other good thing, suddenly it had to come to an end. With competition from Carley's and the lack of parking, Bahlke's Café went out of business.

When it would start getting a little late, with most of the bars closing, it was time to get something to eat before heading for home. We would have a few dimes in our pockets, so across the street we would go to the Skyline Restaurant. How well I remember "Lamb" and Christie behind the steam table dishing up the coneys. It seemed that girls always had to go to the restroom before we ate, which meant a trip through the kitchen and down the steps to the basement. I don't think the Board of Health today would have been too happy with that arrangement. We would have a couple of coneys for a dime each, while the girls would settle for chili spaghetti for a quarter. Sometimes we would have a non-chili eater with us, so we would have to make the trip down to Camp Washington Chili for a hamburger or a double-decker. Then it was time to get on home. As soon as we walked in the door, mom would holler about us being out too late. She could smell the onions and knew we had stopped at the chili parlor on our way home.

We will next visit the Marius Grill at 3832 Glenway Avenue. I know what all who read this are going to say, "Where the heck is Marius Grill?"

MARIUS GRILL
HOME-MADE ICE CREAM
SANDWICHES - GOOD BEER
Short Orders — Fountain Service
3832 GLENWAY AVENUE

Here is betting that some of you have been there many times. If I would have given the address as Glenway and Beech Avenues, you would have known right away. Yes, this location started out being named Carley's, shortly after the end of Prohibition. We can tell by the ad that they served homemade ice cream to get by during Prohibition. For years the sign over one door said Carney's Grill and the other door said Carley's.

A girl graduating from Seton High School really knew she had come of age when exams were over in her senior year. She would head for Carley's back room with a glass of beer in one hand and a cigarette in the other. She was ready to meet the world! You could bet she would return many times, especially on Friday nights. It is also a good bet she might have met her future husband here. In those days, a girl graduating from Seton wasn't too interested in getting a B.A. behind her name. She was more interested in a Mrs. in front of her name.

In 1945, Jimmy and Velma Lyons purchased Carley's. Both were familiar faces around the place but especially on the weekends. Jimmy was behind the bar and Velma was serving up tables in the backroom. About sixteen employees would be helping them out. You may remember sitting in one of the mahogany booths covered with burgundy velvet.

On St. Patrick's Day one could hardly get through the door. The windows were all decked out with shamrocks and the sidewalks were green. Few people know that Crowley's in Mt. Adams was not the first saloon to serve green beer. Several saloons of the day would draw a beer and then have a little green dye put in the glass. But Jimmy had some secret way to actually place the dye in the barrel of beer and when the bartender drew a glass, it came out green from the tap. They really went all out by serving green bread made at St. Lawrence Bakery, along with green hats and horns for everyone!

For some unknown reason, Good Friday was almost as busy as St. Patrick's Day. Maybe because of the good fish sandwich they served. Looking over the menu from those days, a breaded veal cutlet was seventy cents, a piece of homemade pie cost a dime, a shot of Old Grand Dad cost thirty-five cents, a bottle of Royal Amber cost twenty cents and a draft cost a dime. Please, bring back the good old days!

On any given Friday night, especially when Elder had a game, one could hardly move in the back room. One thing you could bet on is that the two Murphy boys, Jim and Bob, would be going head to head and Little Rig's, the bouncer, would have to step-in to keep them in line. As the song on the popular TV show went, "Those Were The Days."

Jim decided to retire and sold out in 1955 to Bob Kramer. The crowd that hung out there over the years suddenly started to get married and it was time to turn it over to a new bunch. Over the next period, several others operated the bar and in the 1990s the business changed and the bar closed. The Eagles took over the place and until this day they still operate, but as a private club.

Next we will stop at the corner of Glenway and Manss Avenues. In 1941, Hoinke Bowling Alley came into being. With 16

lanes, it was one of the finest establishments in the area. Shortly after opening the bowling alley, World War II began. To promote the sale of War Bonds they instituted the "Hoinke Classic" with the top prize of a one thousand dollar bond. I can still remember shopping in the Kroger store which was located on the first floor. When the balls would be rolling down the lanes during league play, it was like you were in a huge thunderstorm.

From this meager beginning, one of the top bowling classics in the country began. In 2008, the payout was over two million dollars. Of course all of this could not have been accomplished on 16 bowling lanes, so after almost thirty years, Hoinke's on Glenway closed and moved to what is now Western Bowl, with 68 lanes. In 2009, there was some talk of tearing this location down to build a shopping center. Thank the Lord, someone came along and Western Bowl was saved. This would have been a terrible loss to the bowling world.

After the bowling alley moved from Glenway and Manss Avenues, the second floor remained vacant for a few years and then came along Shuller's Party Hall. Many wedding receptions were held here. I can remember one in particular that was scheduled for a Saturday night. That afternoon we had a fire in the hall. I

We Teach You
How To "Bowl"

FREE

Ladies and Men Are Invited
—to—

HOINKE - GLENNWAY
ALLEYS

16 ALLEYS . . . Cincinnati's Finest
Manss and Glenway Aves.
WAbash 9500

felt for sure that the heat would affect the huge domed ceiling and it would come down around our necks. But, thanks to the good work of the firefighters, the fire was extinguished before too much damage was incurred. In fact, the happy couple was able to go ahead with their reception that night. For several years after Kroger moved from that location, the downstairs was a smorgasbord restaurant. Today the upstairs remains vacant and the downstairs has become a dollar store.

Gene Rissert's Café and Gardens at 4016 Glenway Avenue was located next door to what was Benders Café at the corner of Glenway and Iliff Avenue. Mr. Rissert ran a family-friendly bar with his Ladies' Sitting Room and garden; he also made the best boiled ham sandwiches. He would buy a great big country ham and then put it in an old lard can. He would boil it slowly, sometimes all day, on the little stove he had in the kitchen. Then when he would slice the ham, the juice would just run out of it. The nurses who worked and lived at the old Dunham Hospital loved to come in for a ham sandwich. It would cost them twenty cents and a Coke cost a nickel. It was quite a break from the meals they were served at the hospital.

Mr. Rissert was also one of those affected when Prohibition hit. As one can see, he turned his saloon into a real estate business. The saloon still operates but the name has been changed to the 51 Bar. With the advent of no smoking in bars today and the garden in the rear no longer in existence, a few chairs have been placed in the side yard; those that desire to smoke can do so outside with their glass of beer.

The Bohemian Lounge at 4100 Glenway Avenue at the corner of Gilsey Avenue was owned by Ray Morano and his wife. It was a nice place to go on a Saturday night and join in the sing-a-long. Our friend, Frank, would bring along his little squeeze box and help the piano player add to the music. As already mentioned, this was the second Bohemian on the Hill. They added Lounge to the name instead of café in order not to confuse people.

Just two doors up the street from the Bohemian, at 4104 Glenway Avenue, we find John Ruby's Café. It later became Pat's Avenue Grill.

Kernan's Bar at 4116 Glenway Avenue, at the corner of Dewey Avenue is the third café that operated in one block along Glenway Avenue. This location later became known as Dewey Grill. Of the three bars, this one caused the most problems. It seemed that the police were always responding to deal with fights and finally it became a haven for druggies. Then, in 2003, the area was declared a nuisance by the city and most of the block was torn down.

Rosemont and Glenway Avenues was for many years the site of the Eagles Hall. Although it was a private club, many dances were held here. On any given Saturday night in the late-1940s or early-1950s, for five bucks one could go and get the best drink-and-drown on the Hill. Along the way you and your date could dance the night away. Over the years, membership in most clubs declined as was the case with the Eagles. They decided to sell the building and move to smaller quarters down the road. No, there was no fire, they just tore the building down and it became a carwash.

You and Your Friends Should Belong to
THE FRATERNAL ORDER OF EAGLES
Price Hill Aerie No. 2203

We now come to French Villa located at 4229 Glenway Avenue at the corner of Winfield Avenue. It was known to many in the late 1930s and early 1940s as Frenchies. Many a serviceman had their last drink here before leaving for service in World War II. Also many enjoyed their first drink home on furlough at Frenchies.

Frenchies attracted a lot of the nurses who worked at Dunham Hospital. They would ride on the bus, or should we say the truck, that came here from the hospital for a night of enjoyment. Shortly after the war ended, Glenway Chevrolet was planning an expansion, and Frenchies ended up becoming the office for them.

With the advent of television and the decline of movie going, the Ackermans, who owned the Sunset Theater at the corner of Glenway and Sunset Avenues, decided to close the theater. Mother Seton Knights of Columbus were looking for a home at the time and decided to buy the theater. They converted it to a meeting hall and a place where wedding receptions and other functions could be held. Over the years, many brides and

grooms had their first dance as a married couple at this location. Many civic events were also held here. Over the years the Price Hill Civic Club held their meetings here, as well as many other functions. But most important, twice a week, bingo players came to enjoy their favorite game. But the bingo games went away, weddings went to fancier locations, and membership rolls started to shrink. It became time for the Knights of Columbus to move on. But, wouldn't you know, Glenway Chevrolet was ready for another expansion! They purchased the building and, after much remodeling, it became their showroom. As time marched on, the building was eventually torn down, making way for the new Carson School building.

We will now skip past Hartung's, which we spent much time on earlier and go to 4406 Glenway Avenue, Katz's Beer Garden. This one really throws a monkey wrench at me. I sure wish there was an old timer around to fill me in on Katz's Beer Garden. You see, the location of Hartung's was 4400 Glenway Avenue, just two doors to the east. It is hard to believe that any two saloons would be operating so close to each other. Looking at the advertisement of the German Band at Katz's Beer Garden, one has to wonder if this could be the remnants of Haberstumpf's Gardens. Oh well, someday someone will come along and fill us in on the details. In any case, it sure must have been a good place to go for some good German music, a nice cold, nickel "Hudey," but most of all for a good limburger sandwich and a hot tamale. I don't know how the tamale got in there. Enough said!

At Prout's Corner there were a few good watering holes. Our first stop will be at Uebel's Bowling Lanes and Grill, later to take on the name of Overlook Bowling Lanes. It was down in the basement at 4904 Glenway Avenue. With six lanes, it was a nice

place for a crowd to get together on a Saturday night and have a bowling party. At a quarter a line and beers for a dime, you and your sweetie could get by for a couple of bucks. But look at what I found in the advertisement on the next page! The Overlook Lunch Room had a full course chicken dinner. The dinner came with a glass of beer for forty-five cents and we could shoot off a few roman candles while we were waiting. Now I am wondering if you were allowed to shoot them off the roof or the sidewalk in front of the building. The thing I liked about the bowling alley was that it had semi-automatic pinsetters; no more placing each pin on that little pin. Now you just had to throw the pins in a basket, pull the lever and they set themselves. Boy, did that ever make it easier on the poor pin boy.

When I was in grade school, Uebel's was a real hangout for the boys from St. Teresa. They had six alleys to play on. We poor guys from the front of the Hill had to be satisfied with only two alleys at Holy Family. Oh well, I guess that is what you get for living in the ghetto!

Just a walk across the street to 4907 Glenway Avenue and you could do a little dancing at the Price Hill Gardens. From the looks of this address, this must have been what was once Woolworth's Five and Ten, now home to Don's Hobby Shop. I don't know if there are many around today who cut a rug here on a Saturday night.

Things start to get a little confusing crossing back over Glenway Avenue. You see, the address for Barry's Tavern was listed as 4914 Glenway. Guerley Inn was listed as 4910, which I know was further out on Glenway Avenue. We will just forget about the address and talk a little about Barry's.

Barry's Tavern was a saloon that served nothing higher than 6% beer. So you would not see too many older whiskey drinkers stopping by there. Mostly a teenage crowd frequented the place, because in those days the legal limit for beer was 18. However, I know a few who might have been several years younger and had a cold one there. Barry's later became The Huddle,

with nice cozy booths. You could stop in after the show at the new Covedale and have a beer and a good sandwich. After The Huddle it became Bella Napoli. Believe me, it was like another Abatico's had suddenly appeared on the Hill! They had the best Italian food, all made from scratch. But the restaurant closed some years back, and it suddenly became a parking lot.

A Friday night with men all dressed in their overalls and the gals with their gingham skirts meant it was "Country Western Night" at Johnnie Leonard's Golden Fleece Lounge. I have to hesitate for a minute and tell you why John went into the saloon business. Here was a guy who for forty or so years finished floors for his mother's Old Reliable Floor Company. After all those years, he decided to become a saloonkeeper. John never made a mistake when applying lacquer to any floor, but one day in a Mt. Auburn house, he forgot to put out the pilot light on the water heater before he got started. Lo and behold, when those fumes hit that pilot light, the result was the biggest fireball anyone wanted to see.

As I rolled down the street in my little red firefighter's car, John was waiting. The first thing he said to me was, "I messed up, Froggy. I forgot the pilot light!"

I told him my men would save the foundation and not to worry. And they were able to put the fire out without too much damage. All John kept saying was, "These fumes must be getting to me; I think I'll try some other business."

Several months later, he was behind the bar at the Golden Fleece. John operated it for six or seven years and then it was time to turn the reins back to Sam. This change resulted in another remodeling job for Price Hill Chili.

While we are in the area of Prout's Corner, we will veer off Glenway Avenue for a few minutes and go to the Ideal Café. It

was located just a few steps off Glenway Avenue at the corner of Cleves Warsaw Pike and Rulison Avenue. It was opened just as Prohibition ended in 1934 by Bud Hotchkiss and, for many years, his son Roy served up the drinks. Nobody seems to know why it was named the Ideal Café. Most who patronized it will say it was far from the ideal place to be. There was no gaudy neon sign to advertise its location, nor any air conditioning to keep the patrons cool. A little black and white television was perched over in the corner, same as the one back when television was a novelty.

One could say that the Ideal Café was a duplicate of many other neighborhood bars that dotted the streets of Price Hill during the 1940s and 1950s. Some were called gin mills, others dives, or even a dump. They were never called what they truly were — home. Certainly they weren't the best of homes, but a refuge to a working man after a long, dull day at some job. It was a place to stop and have a beer with some friends before going home. Going home meant facing a house full of screaming kids and a wife, who had endured the duties of a housewife throughout the day.

The regulars at the Ideal would nod a hello to the bartender and mutter, "Give me a cold one." Sometimes the Ideal would become his den later in the evening, as the children settled into their homework and the wife settled into watching a rerun on their black and white TV set. With a few buddies at the Ideal, he could watch a ballgame or maybe a wrestling match as he squinted at that little black and white TV in the corner. Maybe even a little political debate would take place or a discussion on which high school had the best team. The arguments would get heated but never a fist was raised. Those in attendance knew that a fight could lead to being banished from your favorite watering

The Ideal Cafe, Cleves Pike and Rulison Aves.

hole. After all, those patrons of the Ideal knew they had to find a measure of dignity in the company of other men.

The Ideal Café was the second home to an ex-policeman who was retired and lived only several blocks away. He would get his lawnmower out to cut his grass and, as usual, it would not start. So the right thing to do was to push it up to the Ideal because someone there would know what was wrong with it. And of course, one of the patrons was a mechanic. He would just pull the cord and it would start right away. Off went the poor fellow pushing the running mower down the sidewalk to cut his grass. Several children would look kind of funny at him and ask why he was cutting the sidewalk, but this did not faze him one bit. He was off to cut his lawn and this was what he always did. One of the bar patrons noted, "Guess he will be back next week to have the mower started." Stories like this made hanging in a bar enjoyable.

When the Ideal had been there for twenty-five years, it was felt it was time to celebrate the occasion. So on July 2, 1959, prices were rolled back to what they were when the saloon opened. Beers were a nickel, shots a dime, gallon jugs of beer were seventy cents and ham sandwiches a dime. Some guy would order ten sandwiches and would say to skip the bread on the ninth. As one could imagine, as the word spread, the joint was busy from opening until way past closing time.

The Ideal needed help during this celebration. Marge Frey, who always wanted to be a barmaid, saw this as her golden opportunity. Some women who had waitressed at other places, such as the Cat and the Fiddle, the Hanger, and even the Lookout House, volunteered their services as well.

During this celebration, a stranger came in and ordered a beer and a shot. He laid down a buck and the bartender laid down his change of eighty-five cents. The guy looked funny, picked up his change and hurried out the door, not knowing he could have drank the night away on that buck. Thanks to the people from Schoenling Brewery and a few whiskey salesmen who donated some of the products, the day was fun and the bar did not lose too much.

We will now go back to 4910 Glenway Avenue, the Guerley Inn. Over the years, the genial hosts, Al and Millie, served some of the best food and drinks on the Hill. In 1938, Ed Litmer took over and was he ever good at mixing a drink. The crowds must have poured in to celebrate their reopening because they had to do it again the next Saturday. (I liked the idea of the ladies enjoying their cocktail hour there. Can you just imagine the housewives of those days taking off their aprons about three in the afternoon and heading for the bar? I'll bet that made a lot of husbands happy, when they got home and found no supper on the stove. Maybe that was what led some unhappy husbands looking for Al and Millie.) Suddenly, the sign in the front of the place changed to Price Hill Chili. No more cocktail hours but a lot of chili began to be served along with a few breakfasts.

Along came Sam Beltsos with a chili recipe, and suddenly the air around Prout's Corner was filled with the smell of spices. From a small beginning with a steam table and a few booths, it seemed like every year Sam kept enlarging the place.

Parking was always at a premium at this location. Sam took care of that by tearing down a few buildings. Chili just wasn't going to pay for all the renovations, so the menu was expanded for lunch and dinner, along with the best breakfast in town.

Johnnie Leonard decided to get out of the bar business. Thank the Lord he didn't burn this one down; now Sam could serve

The Guerley Inn

drinks with your favorite meal. Over the years politicians found that when visiting Cincinnati, if you want the West Side vote, you better make a stop at Price Hill Chili. Even Dick Cheney, when he served as Vice President, made a stop here.

One thing any good Westsider knows, if it is Sunday and you want a good breakfast and want to meet a lot of your friends, you better come early. You always had to make sure to bring along your cash, because no charge cards were accepted until the last couple of years. Well, it is a little late and after a night on the Hill, I am afraid my blood alcohol might be over 0.8. I best get a

Price Hill Chili

quarter out of my pocket, hop on the old 35 and take the streetcar to the front of the Hill.

Going back on our tour takes us to Wagner's Beverage Store. It later expanded into what became J & J Café at 5010 Glenway Avenue at the corner of Ferguson Road. As we look at the prices in Wagner's ads, it really makes one's mouth water imagining a case of Jackson 62 beer at $1.20 a case. In today's market one cannot even get a bottle at that price.

It seems like every one of the Maloney boys worked at either the pony keg or the saloon, during their lives. After J & J, the bar

Dick Cheney and a coney! Photo courtesy of the Price Hill Press, October 27, 2004 (and the Price Hill Historical Society art department)

became kind of a hippie joint, with bright lights flashing and the like. I guess the prices caused the pony keg to go by the wayside, because today it's a coffee house.

Across the street was the Colonial Grill at 5031 Glenway Avenue. They were always more about food than drinking. This is now home to Bernens Convalescent Pharmacy Inc.

COLONIAL GRILL
QUALITY FOOD at MODEST PRICES

LUNCHEONS   DINNERS   SANDWICHES

5031 GLENWAY AVENUE   Phone Wabash 9593

At 5077 Glenway, we come to Streibig's, a neighborhood bar owned by Charlie Streibig. When Steve McLaughlin took this over in the late 1970s, it became sort of an Irish Pub similar to the "Cheers" bar on television. The ancient Order of Hibernians kind of made it their place to hang out, with a lot of green flags, especially on St. Patrick's Day. Bob Farrell, a retired firefighter, hung out here and loved to draw pictures as he would see patrons come into the bar. If you stopped by and he happened to be there, the next time you came back your picture might be hanging on the wall. Over the years some three hundred heads hung on the walls. One could say that this saloon was a family art gallery. Years passed on; both Steve and Bob are gone. The crowds in the bar got a little rowdier, much to the displeasure of the police and the neighbors. With the threat of the loss of their licenses, the

90

owners cleaned up their act and the bar is back in business.

The Corner Pub

Our next stop is Peggy's Grill; although they served beer, they probably served far more cherry cokes, with all the teenagers that frequented the place. It was located at 5259 Glenway Avenue. There are very few who attended Western Hills, Seton, or Elder high schools sometime during the 1930s, 1940s or early 1950s who didn't stop by there for a double-decker and a cherry Coke. One thing was for sure, if you were younger than eighteen, you had better not ask for a beer or Smitty would be all over you. It was the favorite place for girls to get a handful of nickels and start calling up guys for a date for the senior dance; no such thing as a prom in those days. (Who would have had enough money to rent a tux?) If things got

Peggy's Grill, in the Forties

a little wild, Smitty would block the front door, so you couldn't get out, while Peggy called the cops. We always knew you could go to the basement men's room and jump out the window.

All in all, after a night at the Covedale, it was not too far a walk with your favorite girl to have a little food at Peggy's Grill. You always knew you would meet some of your friends there. Peggy's is long gone but the building became the Hitching Post and then Lutz Flowers, a florist shop.

A few years ago, I went into the flower shop and said to the clerk, "If this place could only talk." She looked at me funny. I then told her about the good times we had in the past. She was really surprised to know that it once was the biggest hangout for high school students on the Hill.

Note: Just as I have finished writing this book, the building that was once Peggy's Grill, the Hitching Post and Lutz Flowers at 5259 Glenway Avenue, was razed. Only memories remain!

This completes our trek along Glenway Avenue. We also had a few popular bars that were on side streets. First we must make our way back to Prout's Corner and pick up at a bar that is kind of a mystery to all.

In 1933, we find an advertisement for Haggerty's Tavern located on Cleves Warsaw Pike, between Rulison and Coronado Avenues. In searching for buildings that could have been the location of this saloon, those who lived in the neighborhood could only suggest a small building that later became Boone Storage. But, from the look of the waiter in the Haggerty's Tavern ad serving up those frosty nickel and dime beers, it must have been a pretty ritzy place.

We will now go back to the front of the Hill, near the corner of Hawthorne and Price Avenues, a short distance from Holy Family School. In 1932, Gus Wagner owned an icehouse at 3108 Price Avenue. He delivered ice to homes throughout the neighborhood. The housewife didn't even have to be home. She usually left the kitchen door open and had a little sign she displayed in her window, letting Gus know how much ice she needed. He would enter the house, put the ice in her icebox, and collect the money next time around.

PRICE HILL'S MOST UNIQUE

BEER GARDEN

Open Day & Night

Serving Draught Beer - - - **5c** and **10c**

CHICKEN AND FISH SANDWICHES

A-Specialty

Haggerty's Tavern

CLEVES PIKE NEAR GLENWAY
Between Rulison and Coronado

In 1934, with the end of Prohibition, Gus Wagner decided with Harvey Pfau to open a saloon at 3103 Price Avenue. There was a barbershop in front and the bar was in the rear. Later that year the barber left and they took over the whole store. In 1935, Gus bought out Harvey Pfau and named the bar Wagner's Café.

Bill Sieve, who operated a bar opposite Holy Family School before Prohibition, became the day bartender and John Drack and Big Herm Von Uhm became the night bartenders. Sis Overbeck was the waitress and Ray Berding played the piano.

The grand opening of Gus Wagner's Pony Keg was during the Depression and a night out was probably to the neighborhood saloon for a few nickel beers. Gus was well known by all those in the neighborhood, as he continued delivering his ice.

Knothole baseball was in its infancy. Gus liked baseball and sponsored several teams, some of which went-on to win city tournaments. Several members of the Reds lived in the neighborhood during the season and, to the delight of all the youngsters, would stop by the café for a beer after their games. Some of these

Grand **OPENING**

GUS WAGNER'S PONY LEG STATION
FRIDAY AUGUST 12, 1938

93

included Ernie Lombardi, Eddie Joost, and Paul Derringer. Paul was good for bringing a ball along to the café. Sometimes Gus would give the ball to one of the local kids.

At Wagner's Café, there was always a little steam table in the front window with a pot of soup or chili on it. The bartender began putting some of the chili on the hot dogs and calling them Coney Islands. I believe that the Coney Island sandwiches were first introduced in this area at Wagner's Cafe.

In 1946, Gus Wagner decided to move onto bigger things and bought Woodlawn Hall. John Drach and Big Herm moved on with him. Bill Bates bought the Wagner's Café and renamed it Bates Café. Bill Sieve stayed on as the day bartender. Bill's brother-in-law, Harold Mitchell, along with Harry Hartman, became night bartenders. Sis became a fixture as the waitress.

Then Walter Lee, along with his son Harry, took over the bar and renamed it Lee's Café in 1950. Harry Hartman, along with Paul Harmon, Tom Hess, and Earl Williams, became bartenders. Bill Sieve stayed on until he retired in 1952. Over the years, one runs into good bartenders, but it is seldom you run into one you can call excellent. Bill Sieve fit this bill! He knew every customer who walked through the door. He knew what they drank and, by the look on their faces, whether they were having a good day or a bad one.

94

When Walter Lee's other son turned twenty-one, he also began working at the bar. In 1960, the two brothers decided it was time for dad to retire and they bought him out. In 1970, Harry

Lee's Café, 3103 Price Avenue

bought out his brother, Jack, who was ready to give other work a try. Then, in 1977, Harry too decided he had enough of the bar business and sold out. He went to work at the courthouse. One might say he went from one bar to another!

After the Lee family, several others operated the saloon and in the early-2000s the bar closed. Since the late 1970s, the neighborhood has seen many changes. It's no longer safe to leave your back door open, as in the days when Gus Wagner made his ice deliveries.

As a youngster, much of my time revolved around Elberon Avenue near Mt. Echo Park, as well as the little shopping area near Elberon Avenue and Bassett Road. Here we had a barber, deli, and drycleaner, but most important to us was an auto repair shop run by a man named Phil. If a chain came off our bike, Phil would always put it back on. If we needed a bolt for our wagon, he would say to go over and look in the box for one. Suddenly one day in the summer of 1937, after the great flood, we saw Phil's little shop being torn down. We rushed to ask Gus, the barber, what was going on. He told us they were tearing the garage down so some man could build a saloon.

"Oh, no! You mean Phil is going to be gone?"

"No," said Gus. "He's moving into the gas station up the street." Over the next several weeks, work began on the new building. As the joists were put up for the roof, some of us kids used to get up and play on them at night, after the workers had left. Soon the building was completed. Late in the summer of 1937, Mr. Jaspers opened a saloon called the Mt. Echo Tavern at 481 Elberon Avenue. Since this was still the time during the Depression, we all wondered where Mr. Jaspers got all the money to build a saloon. You see, there was already a saloon in the neighborhood, Mary's House. But with so many people going to Mt. Echo Park, it looked as if maybe another saloon might make it around there.

Then came spring and a lot of our older brothers were not working. So, the hangout was in the park. It came time for softball and they got a team together, but they needed a sponsor. They asked the barber, but things were not too good with him. Then they asked Mr. Jaspers, and he agreed to sponsor their team.

Our brothers usually played several nights at Mt. Echo Park. After the games, they would go to Mt. Echo Tavern. Most of the boys, without a job and little money, would sit out in the rear yard of the tavern among the empty barrels and beer cases. Mr. Jaspers would always bring out a few pitchers of beer. As youngsters, we were the batboys, so he would always give us a bottle of pop. Over the next several years, things continued on like this. Then the war came along and we saw many of these guys getting jobs or going into the army.

Suddenly one day in early 1942, while walking by the Mt. Echo Tavern, I noticed the door was closed and there was a wreath on the door. As usual, we rushed into the barbershop to ask Gus what had happened. He told us Mr. Jaspers had died. He was our good friend, so we were very sad. We wondered what would happen to the saloon, as it was the only one left in the neighborhood since Mary's House had gone out of business.

Soon we saw the saloon was open again and we came to know Mrs. Jaspers and her son Bob, who were now running it. We soon found out that Bob was going into the

---

Mt. Echo Tavern

BEER - WINE - WHISKEY

TELEVISION

453 Elberon Avenue

MT. ECHO PONY KEG

481 ELBERON

WA 7485

3.2% and 6% BEER
WINES — SOFT DRINKS — MIXERS
FREE DELIVERY SERVICE

BOB JASPERS

Red Jaspers

army and Mrs. Jaspers would be alone. We were in high school now and our friends stretched further than grade school. We got to know kids from other schools. Her son, Red, was one of them and the next thing we knew, he was tending bar after school to help out his mom. Red was only a sophomore at Elder High School at the time. Here he was, tending bar at the age of fifteen or sixteen. How could this be?

One must remember that this was during the war. Many were working in war factories and some ladies became know as "Rosie the Riveter." Kids from Elder and a lot of other schools were doing all kinds of jobs. During this time a lot of Red's friends started to come into the bar to help stock the coolers, and they also might have sneaked a cold one once in awhile. They were also doing jobs usually held by older men, such as working in factories, trucking freight for railroads, and even playing major league baseball. That is what Joe Nuxall (the famous Cincinnati Red's pitcher who became the Red's radio commentator) did and became the youngest ballplayer in history. Maybe we can say Red Jaspers, becoming a bartender at age fifteen, was the youngest bartender in history!

Soon the war was over and Red's brother Bob was back home. Things started to get back to normal. Many people were doing their drinking at home, as they enjoyed their television, but they had to take care of their thirst. Bob and Red now opened Mt. Echo Pony Keg. They would deliver your drinking needs right to

Elberon Country Club

your home. For the next forty years or so, Red and Bob continued the business. As they got older, it was time to look for something easier to do. They both ended up at the courthouse, the same as Harry Lee. Again, from one bar to the other! After they sold the saloon, it kept operating for the next ten or so years with a variety of owners. As was the case with Lee's, the neighborhood changed, the crowd changed, and soon the Mt. Echo Tavern and Pony Keg was history.

Before completing our saloon tour throughout Price Hill, we must mention a place where, most likely, alcohol was consumed, before and during Prohibition. However, one could not call it a saloon. This establishment was Price Hill's Elberon Country Club. It was located on the Hill's highest point, with fairways stretching clear to Glenway Avenue and Rapid Run Road. It was the forerunner to the Western Hills Country Club. Today, the location of the clubhouse (it's the same old building, though significantly remodeled) is the Liberty Mission Baptist Church at 1009 Overlook Avenue.

Some of the "rich and famous" of Price Hill could be seen at Elberon Country Club. One has to wonder if George Remus, our famous bootlegger, ever shot a few rounds here, since he lived on Hermosa Avenue only a block from the golf course. If so, one could imagine him probably bringing along a few bottles of his "medicine" to be shared with fellow golfers. By the way, his property was part of the beer baron Henry Lackman's estate.

THE OUTER LIMITS

The many saloons throughout Price Hill lined the streets of the community for years. Of course there were also some saloons located just beyond the limits of the Hill, where residents and non-residents alike also stopped to have a few drinks.

I have great memories of Quebec Gardens, located at the foot of Quebec Road. Over the years they were noted for the good food they served and as a place to party and dance. Many wedding receptions were held there. On any given Saturday night, many from the Hill could be seen waltzing across the dance floor with their favorite girlfriends. However, if you were stag, the boys from Fairmount did not take too kindly to you stealing the girls from "Little Italy." If things got too chummy, you had to be prepared to fight your way out of the place.

Eddie Rauh, who owned the place, also served as the bouncer. He was known to hit with his wrist instead of his fist. One blow from him and your head really began to twirl. In later years, a group of firefighters bought the place and renamed it Western Gardens, with a taste of down-home music. After operating for several years, they found that putting out a fire was a much easier job and decided to close. Then it became a Chinese restaurant, serving some of the best Chinese food around. Now it has closed and the building is vacant.

One can't overlook the Roller Grille, located on Ferguson Road. It was next to the Western Hills Rollatorium, which for a time was one of the best roller rinks in the area. Oh, how I used to hate those guards who could skate so good backwards and get all the girls. On any given night after roller skating was finished, the Grille would be filled with a bunch of teenagers drinking their cokes and having a sandwich. However, during the daytime the place was quite different. It would suddenly become one of the biggest horse-betting parlors in the area. A stranger walking in from the street would certainly think he was in a modern day betting parlor in Las Vegas. Blackboards lined the walls, with listings of races at various tracks throughout the country. The speaker on the wall blasted out "They're at the post at Monmouth!" The betters would hurry to the window to make their bets.

The betting activities taking place at the Roller Grille were possible because it was on a small strip of land that was outside the city limits. So you see, it was not under police jurisdiction and apparently, at the time, the county just ignored this activity. Then the war came along and the owner of the roller rink turned it into a factory. War materials were made here and were probably far more profitable than skating; the roller rink and the Grille disappeared.

The Ranch Turf and Gun Club at Sidney and Anderson Ferry Roads was yet another place where one could find betting as the big draw. Maybe the Turf part of their name was right, but it is doubtful that much trapshooting went on there. After being closed for several years it reopened with a new name, the Pirate's Den. The front entrance resembled a Pirate Ship. They certain-

Tank Martin's, somewhere in the railroad yard

101

ly saved on their electric bill because inside the place was kept pretty dark. A patron stated that you could easily cheat on your girlfriend in this place; she could walk in and never know you were there. The Pirate's Den moved out to a shopping center on Werk Road not too long ago, and their old building is empty.

Tank Martin's After-Hours Bar is not known to many on the Hill. It is difficult to give a location for this place, because it was in the middle of the C & O Railroad yards, which is now Glencrossing Shopping Center. But if 2:30 a.m. was not a late enough hour to go home, you could always make your way to "Tank's" for one last drink. It wasn't fancy, just a few tables and chairs spread throughout an old concrete block building. The heating system consisted of a giant fireplace in which old railroad ties were burnt. Mom always knew where I had been when I came home smelling of creosote smoke.

Another outer limits saloon was Eddie's Tavern at 408 Greenwell Avenue. It was said that if you were not in your mother's arms and you could say "Give me a beer," you were old enough to drink at Eddie's. Maybe that is stretching the point a little bit, but one thing you could bet, as soon as dad would let you drive the car, you and a group of your friends would make your way to Eddie's.

You see, at that time (early-1950s) Delhi had no police, just a constable patrolling the place. So, you can bet he was never going to bother Eddie. After Eddie left, Jack Maloney became the bartender. Everyone knew Jack from J and J's. Suddenly most of his drinkers headed for Delhi. Jack passed on but his name lives on, as Maloney's is the name of that bar today.

In those early days, we looked at Delhi as being way out in the country. The kids that came to Elder from Delhi "came by way of horse and buggy." Their biggest industry, as far as I was concerned, was Elsasser's Farm. It was not The Farm we know as the party hall today, but the one where you went with a gallon jug. That jug was for filling with milk, not with beer. Steve, who ran the place, was blind. He only had to meet you once, hear your voice, and he would know who you were the next time you made a visit.

If it was a hot Sunday summer night and you did not feel like spending the night in some stifling bar, you could always make your way to either Green's Woods or Lauterbach's Grove in Delhi and enjoy a few free beers. Yes, I said free! You see, this was always a great place for political candidates to do a little campaigning. All you had to do was hang around the bar for a minute and you would hear the bartender yell out, "Twenty-one beers on Mayor Jimmy Stewart."

PRICE HILL CIVIC CLUB

ANNUAL

FAMILY PICNIC

SUNDAY

August 8th

LAUTERBACH GROVE

(Greenwell and Delhi Pike)

Free Transportation from 8th and Pedretti

5¢ Ham Sandwich 5¢
Turtle Soup
Hot Dogs

HUDEPOHL BEER ON TAP

Nieman Printers

As he would set up the beers, you could just grab one and start drinking. You would soon come to find out that out of a six-ounce mug of beer you might get about three ounces of beer; the rest would be foam. If you would add to this the fact that you were drinking "Picnic Beer," you were lucky to come up to 3.2% of alcohol.

Don't worry though; Jimmy's opponent was not going to be outdone by him. It wouldn't take long before the bartender would announce that the opponent was also setting up the house. Again, out there in Delhi at that time, the constable was not going to bother you. However, you had better mind your manners because he did not like anyone fighting in his township.

NEW KIDS ON THE HILL

We would be remiss if we failed to mention the bars that have come along in the past ten years. For a time, many seem to be located along a one-block stretch of Crookshank Road. It kind of reminds you of the many bars that were located along a similar stretch of Warsaw Avenue. Looking at Applebee's and O'Charley's, we would have to classify these as franchised bars,

known more for their food than for drinking. Although they do have a nice bar area and many patrons occupying the area, they are mostly waiting to be seated at a table or intent on watching some sporting event. One has to wonder how they can concentrate on any one game, since several different channels are on various televisions with a different game on each. It sure is a long way from the 1940s, when you used to watch a game on a little ten-inch black and white TV in the corner bar.

Our next visit is Champions Grille, opened by Dr. O'Connor and several westside high school friends. He is an avid sports fan for sure. You better be wearing purple when you go in on a night that Elder is playing. His interest in baseball also brought the Cincinnati Steam team to the Hill, playing their home games just up the street at the new Western Hills High School baseball field. Again, with all the TVs (they advertise 40 televisions) in the place, there is no way you can miss your favorite team playing. As the sign on the wall says, "Good Food, Good Drinks, Good Friends."

Note to the Reader: Again, just as I've finished writing about Champions Grille, it has closed at the Crookshank location, but reopened recently in the shopping center out on Glenway across from the Western Hills Plaza, near the new Pirate's Den.

Patrick's Sports Bar is on the other side of the street on Crook-shank. The Hill would not be complete without having one bar designated as a "Sports Bar." Maybe most of the sports people get here early in the morning before they go to play a round of golf. Some say they have a breakfast menu that is equal to that at Price Hill Chili. They must also serve good drinks during happy hour, because the parking lot always seems to be full.

A NIGHT OUT ON THE TOWN

Price Hill boys may have stayed close to the saloons on the Hill during the weeknights, but come the weekend, they were ready for a night on the town. So they would put on a tie and a coat and hit the night spots with their best girlfriend. With the war on and gasoline being rationed, the means of transport usually became the Warsaw 35 streetcar. There couldn't have been a better place for entertainment than the block of Fifth Street, south of the Tyler-Davidson Fountain.

The Gibson Hotel took up most of the block. You could either spend a night bowling in the basement or go to the top floor and dance to some of the best bands in the land. A popular bar, the 31 Bar, would serve some really great drinks. This bar also proved to be popular with the young ladies on Saturday afternoons, after a round of shopping downtown. They always knew a stop here would result in finding some of their friends.

A real treat was the Albee Theatre at the west end of the block. For eighty cents, you could see a first-class stage show with the likes of maybe Bing Crosby or Frank Sinatra, and after that, a first-run movie. Just to walk into the Albee and up the grand staircase made one feel as if you were in some plush nightclub. After the show, you and your date could make your way to either the Cricket or Wiggins for a drink and a late night snack. Both of these locations had a Price Hill connection, as they were owned by the Elsasser family, who owned much of the land in the area of the present St. William Church. If it was getting late and the bars were closing, a stop at the Purple Cow would get you a late night snack or an early breakfast. If you were Catholic, you could even catch the "Printers' Mass" at St. Louis Church. Then you could catch the "Owl" streetcar and have your date home by three a.m. and sleep-in the next day. The whole night-out for you and your date only cost you about five bucks; this even allowed you a quarter to drop in the collection basket at church.

If it was a special Saturday night, there was no wasting it on a movie downtown. Maybe it was your sweetheart's birthday, or maybe your number came up in the draft and you were off to the Army in a week or so. Dad would lend us the car in those kinds of situations, so we could spread our wings a little further. Off we would go over the river and up Dixie Highway to the Lookout House. We would have our choice of having dinner and going to a show, or maybe just listening to the piano player in the Little Club on the first floor. Whatever it was we did, we learned new words that we seldom would hear today. If it was a good show upstairs, terms like "Cover Charge or Minimum" would be the rule of the day. If the show was of top caliber, a cover charge or admission cost would always be levied. If there was

just a comedian performing, the minimum would be charged, meaning we would have to eat and drink so much to cover the amount. Before we would leave, we would go into the gambling room and stick a few nickels in the slot machine.

Our choice was not limited only to the Lookout House. We could have driven up the long driveway to Beverly Hills or maybe even stopped by the Latin Quarter. You see, in those days, Las Vegas had nothing on our area. We had some of the finest nightclubs in the land right here, as well as top shows performing at them. If we chose not to make the trip across the river, we could drive out Reading Road to Castle Farm in Roselawn, where they had good shows and dancing, but no slots.

Going to the movies on a Saturday night in today's world means going to a big box where seven or eight features are showing in little cubicles. The drink of choice is a giant-size soda along with a larger box of popcorn. Your feet end up being glued to the floor, thanks to the last person who sat in the seat and spilled the giant soda all over the floor. Or maybe if you would like to dance, your trip across the river will take you to "The Levee" in Newport. Again, the dance halls there resemble a large box. If you want to catch a stage show, you can make your way down the river to one of the casinos. Now, instead of dropping a few nickels in the slots, you can play the popular penny machines. Oh boy, bring back the good old days!

Sunday nights were a little less formal, and with work the next day, one didn't want to be staying out too late. So, maybe it was a trip to Kern Aylward's place on Main Street in Covington, now known as Mainstrasse. Kern, having been from the acting field, always seemed to attract a few professionals who would belt out a few tunes. The most fun on Sunday night was amateur night. Anyone could take the mike and act like they were a professional singer. The best of all was this guy that sang the song, "The Stutterer." He would have the house roaring. To this day I have never heard this song again. And, by the way, one always had to make sure they made a visit to Kern's on St. Patrick's Day. Here the Irish music and green beer flowed from early morn until late at night.

Ault Park Pavilion

Another fun place to visit was the "Tally Ho" on McMillian Street in Walnut Hills. The parking lot was changed into a summer garden. Draft beers were only fifteen cents, so it was not too costly to send a round of drinks to the table of girls that were sitting across from you. It was a nice way to strike up a conversation and maybe even pick up a date for the next weekend.

If dancing was your thing on a Sunday night, the place to go was Ault Park. One just couldn't beat the price anywhere in town. It cost a dime for a dance. If you were on a date, about five dances were usually the limit. You could also get a bottle of Weideman beer for a quarter. So, for about two and a half bucks one could really have an enjoyable night dancing and drinking under the stars.

The whole Coney Island scene was a special time. First of all, it would all begin in the springtime with the moonlight cruises on the Island Queen. High school fraternities and sororities could sponsor a night and pick up a few bucks for their treasury. The cost for the cruise was a dollar, with the sponsoring group getting a quarter for each ticket they sold. The cruises usually lasted about three hours, with some really good bands and singers. The most popular performer was Clyde Trask, who usually packed the dance floor. When things got too hot, you could always ask your date to get a little fresh air on the top deck. Many a guy or girl got their first kiss on the top deck of the Island Queen.

On a Saturday night during the summer, it was time to head for Moonlite Gardens. Again, some of the best bands played here, such as Barney Rapp. You would really feel like you were in a high-class nightclub. But, best of all, you could bring your own bottle of spirits and buy a few mixers, so it was another place where the night was not that expensive.

Regardless of how hard you worked on Tuesdays or how early you had to go in on Wednesdays, you should not miss going to the Gardens on Tuesday night. You see, Tuesday was ladies' night, so the girls got in free while the boys had to pay. But believe me, even though it was a journey across town, the Price Hill guys were there en masse. Many couples met there and their relationships lasted throughout their lives.

Oh, there were other places; just maybe not as popular as those already mentioned. You could usually find a few Price Hillians no matter where you went, such as at the Wine Cellar in Silverton, Ohio. What a headache the next day! There was Mecklenburg Garden for a taste of German Beer or even the St. Bernard Eagles Hall for a few dances. But come the work week, it was back to the bars on the Hill we knew so well.

The Island Queen

Moonlight Gardens

BAR FACTS

In days gone by, there were tools that every bartender had to have. One was a little plastic spatula that he used to cut the foam off a glass of beer. The perfect collar was about one half inch of foam. A patron drinking his beer would know that it wasn't flat if a small amount of foam remained in the glass as he finished his drink.

Another tool was a short rubber hose, which was used in filling a gallon jug. The beer would first flow into the lower portion of the jug, not creating too much foam. To attempt to fill a jug without this rubber hose, the jug would usually fill with nothing but foam. Price Hill patrons carried a gallon jug to their favorite tavern, asking for a half gallon of beer. They knew the bartender would usually fill the jug three-quarters full. Some patrons would even know to carry two jugs, asking the bartender to fill both half full. As the bartender would look at them kind of funny, they always had the excuse that they were taking the other jug home for a neighbor. Some bartenders even had a little ruler and would measure the amount of beer in the jug. True Price Hillians soon learned to bypass these bars.

"Happy Men" was the term used for brewery salesmen, who visited saloons and bought the house a round of drinks. The best of these salesmen was Peck Haverkamp, who worked for Hudepohl Brewery over the years. Peck didn't care whether you were drinking his beer, or even a shot, he always said, "Give them what they want."

Many salesmen would have the bartender set up only the kind of beer they were distributing, however. There was a popular myth that went through many bars on the Hill. The story goes that if the bartender saw a salesman coming, he would put a broom outside by the front door of the saloon. That indicated to the bar regulars in the neighborhood that this was a chance to get a free beer. They'd make their way in haste to the bar for their free drink.

Barrels of beer were usually stored in a cooler in the basement of the saloon. Thus, the beer flowed some distance from the barrel in the basement to the tap. Over time these lines would get residue in them and the beer would have a sour taste. In order to avoid this problem, it was imperative that these lines be flushed often. Usually a man would visit the saloon each week with a little pump. He would pump a solution through the lines to prevent them from building up a residue.

Some saloons, having their coolers on the same floor as the bar, would advertise that their beer flowed directly from the barrel to the tap. They usually had false barrelheads with the tap coming right out of them, with no lines, no residue, and only fresh beer.

In order to build up attendance, it was popular for some clubs and even churches to serve beer after their meetings. Some clubs would charge a buck or so; maybe even have a split-the-pot raffle. Members found this a nice way to have a night out and drink a few beers on the cheap. The Price Hill Civic Club, West Price Hill's community council, has continued to carry on this tradition of having beer at their meetings. Even today, many a politician will show up at the meetings knowing he can meet a few constituents while enjoying a cold one. Another good example of Price Hillians enjoying their beer is "Dad's Club" at Elder High School. For the past forty years or so, this club has gathered on Tuesday nights, during football and basketball season, to review the game films of past weeks. They are known to enjoy a good night by downing a few cold ones and throwing in a few bucks. Their endeavors go beyond this night. Over the years they have contributed thousands to the Elder athletic program.

Old beer signs, such as those of the neon type, have been prized items that hang in basement rathskellers. Even chairs (one may even find old seats from Crosley Field), glasses, or the like, are treasured by many. Probably the largest collection of Hudepohl Beer memorabilia belongs to a Price Hill resident by the name of Gene Felix. For years his father labored at the brewery, so Gene had a liking for the company that put food on their table. His collection contains just about every item ever distributed by the brewery, and also includes many pictures. He has been happy to show his display to many.

A good bartender would always look out for his customers. When one had a few too many drinks, he would ask someone to see that the customer got home safely. One soon learned to take the advice of the sign that hung in the pool hall and bar that Joe Brauer ran on Enright Avenue. (The sign is shown on the next page.) The subject of the sign is an unsuspecting soul, who when taking a customer home, lingered on the porch too long after ringing the bell. The housewife appeared with broom in hand and after giving her husband a few good whacks, she took out after the Good Samaritan. Her thinking was that he had been responsible for getting her husband inebriated. From that time on, he knew to set the drunk on the front porch and then quickly follow the advice on Joe's sign and "Run Like Hell."

WHEN I'M FULL TAKE ME HOME

Name —————————————

Address ————————————

RING THE BELL

RUN LIKE HELL

JOE BRAUER
937 ENRIGHT AVE.

Billiard   *Beer*

MEMORIES ON A FINAL SPIN
PAST OLD SALOONS

A friend of mine, Buddy, was in town for the Christmas holidays. He called and asked if, for old times' sake, I would like to hit a few bars on the Hill. I told him I haven't had anything to drink stronger than a "city highball" (that's tap water for those of you who don't know the lingo) for several years, but it would be a nice time to go for a ride to see just what bars are still in operation on the Hill.

Ballinasloe ◊ E/J Bar: We made our way down Glenway Avenue on our way to Lower Price Hill, passing what use to be Ballinasloe. I noticed the sign on front of the building was E/J Bar. We pulled the car over and went to see if they were still in operation. The first thing we noticed was a big padlock on the front door. As we peered through the window, we could see the old bar that Mr. Coney usually stood behind. On the bar were piled boxes of used clothing. Throughout the rest of what was the barroom, tables were strewn ad clothing was thrown all over the floor. My friend said, "Boy, if Mr. Coney is looking down from above, I don't think he's too happy."

"Yep, he used to keep that back bar so nice and polished. It looks like the last day that E/J was in operation there must have been some kind of brawl in the place. Mr. Coney sure didn't allow any fights in there!"

Sportsman Bar: We made our way down to the foot of the Hill. It was quite a job explaining to my friend that the Sportsman Bar was in Lower Price Hill. To him, this area was always known as "Eighth and State." I told him that the city administration divided the city into fifty-two neighborhoods, thus Price Hill became Lower, East, and West. His remark to me was that there always were a bunch of crazies who ran City Hall, and I had to kind of agree. We pulled the car to the curb in the front of the Sportsman Bar. Again we were met with a big padlock on the door. In the past, a padlocked door meant that the saloonkeeper had violated some liquor law and an agent had shut them down for a time.

Peering in the window at the Sportsman Bar, we saw the same thing as we had just seen at E/J Bar. It appeared again that on the last night it was open, a bunch of "hardy drinkers" had really had a brawl. Tables and chairs were laying everywhere with a few bottles and glasses mixed in. Over its years of operation, the old Sportsman Bar saw a few good brawls, so it probably was only right that it went out in glory with one last brawl.

Standing by the curb in front of the bar, we surveyed the neighborhood and reminisced about what it looked like in days gone by. The Sportsman Bar building was the only business still standing. Across the street, Sols's Department Store and the Neihaus Shoe Store once stood. Now it's a vacant lot. My friend commented on how his mother used to bring him down on the Incline and they would do all their shopping here.

Yes, there were restaurants, a candy shop, several grocery stores, and the like. One didn't have to worry about going to a shopping mall or not having an automobile. It only cost five cents to ride the Incline down to Eighth and State to do all your shopping right there.

The bank that stood on the corner was still there. It looks pretty good, but it is no longer used as a bank. From the looks of the houses remaining in the neighborhood, there probably wouldn't be enough customers to keep it open. Oh yes, there is a Health Center. It seems that today every neighborhood needs one of these. In the old days, we had enough doctors and dentists to take care of people. My friend reminded me of the time during the 1937 flood when we had to walk down to the corner library to get a shot so that we wouldn't get diphtheria. After all, with no water coming out of the faucets, we had to drink spring water from the ground.

Primavista: Our next stop was back on top of the Hill. I told Buddy that if the Incline was still operating, we could jump on it and be at the Primavista Restaurant in a matter of minutes. Oh well, we will make our way up the Hill on Warsaw Avenue like the many funeral corteges that made their way up the Hill. Thank the Lord we were in a car and not in a horse and buggy going past "Dead Man's Curve!"

We entered Queen's Tower and on the lower level we went into the Primavista. We were greeted by Frank and Jean Lenkerd, the owners. Over the years they have been active in the community, and if your group was having a fundraiser, you could rest assured that they would kick in with something. On Thanksgiving in 2009, the Price Hill Parade Committee honored them by making them the Grand Marshals of the Annual Thanksgiving Day Parade.

116

As we made our way up the Hill, I had to tell Buddy not to order the spaghetti, though. I told him that here it comes with not only a few meatballs, but also a higher price than he might be expecting. The only spaghetti he knew came with a topping of chili and a little cheese. Instead, he ordered a beer and I had a glass of ice water with a piece of lemon in it. We sat right at the window and marveled at the view. He said he doesn't think there's a better view from any spot in the city. I agreed! You can see clear down to Bromley in Kentucky, all the way past the new Reds ballpark, and, on a clear day, you can even see the water tower in Mt. Washington.

We looked off to the side of the building, now called Olden View Park. Buddy reminded me of the old Incline House that once stood on the spot. Many times we rode our bicycles out through that building after getting off the Incline. Oh, how the women who were on the Incline car used to get so mad at us when our bike pedals would brush against their stockings. One day I thought old Elsie was going to beat us up with her pocketbook after tearing a runner in her good silk stockings.

We kept reminiscing about those days and when the Incline quit operating in 1943. Some church began using the Incline House. All of us neighborhood kids went in that church to "get saved" one night. Everything went okay until Hal started to laugh. We all got ushered out the door as the preacher told us, "You just got Unsaved!"

Hock's Café: The radio tower still stands next to where the Incline House building was. We were remembering those steeple jacks as they were building the tower. They would climb up and down that tower as if they were a bunch of cats. Then one day, one of them fell and got killed. As was their ritual, they all quit working that day and went over to Hock's Café and got drunk. But, they were back on the job the next morning, as if nothing had happened the day before.

Holy Family Gym: We made our way down Eighth Street and stopped at Holy Family Gym. It was a Friday night and, as usual, the ladies were bowling. Few people know that this is probably one of the oldest operating bowling alleys in the state of Ohio. There is a picture in the back room of "Ortman's Five," who were champions of the Price Hill League in 1914, when they bowled at Holy Family. I would imagine the alleys were operating even before that. It seems it will soon be time for the Gym to celebrate its one hundredth birthday.

The place was crowded as usual on a Friday night, usually because of a basketball tournament in the downstairs gym. But, on this particular night, the Pipe Covers were having their annual Christmas party, and the drinks and the food were flowing freely, as always at these parties over the years. And, wouldn't you know it, Buddy, during his working days, was in the building trades. Many of those he worked with have passed on, but on this night many of their sons were in attendance. The old stories about days on the job of building Cincinnati flowed along with the beer that Buddy was consuming. I settled for a bottle of pop. There is nothing like that little bottle of Wagner's Vichy, which many of us would drink during Lent, when we laid off beer.

Several guys were shooting pool and as usual, trying to make a shot off the rail. The ball bounced off the table and across the floor. I could hear the ghost of Eddie (the bartender) hollering, "Take it easy over there!"

We made our way into the back room, where all the pictures of past athletes hang along the wall with the many trophies filling the cases. Over the years, it was noted throughout the city that Holy Family put out some of the best athletes. Also, many clubs made the Gym their home and held their meetings here.

Buddy had to bring up the night one of these clubs, the Troubadours, were having one of their meetings and our friends, Yake and Fritz, decided to have a pretzel fight. A box of pretzels had been left over from a party the Saturday night before. I can still hear Eddie screaming as he came into the room, "You're all out for two weeks!"

Eddie threw many individuals out for two weeks, but I guess the Troubadours were the only club with all of its members banned from the Gym for two weeks.

I noticed Buddy pouring a few more down as he talked with the sons of many of those he used to work with. I decided it was definitely time for us to be hitting the road. Good thing I was driving. If he was at the wheel and we got pulled over, I knew for sure he would blow close to 2.0. His wife was waiting for him at her sister's house. Best I remember the sign that hangs in Joe Brauer's Pool Hall, "When I'm full, take me home, ring the bell, run like hell!" I pulled in front of the house, helped him up on the porch, rang the bell and ran like hell. "See you tomorrow, Buddy!"

Surprisingly, the next day Buddy called and was ready to continue on our journey. As I picked him up, I noticed his eyes were kind of bloodshot from his bout with beer the night before. He mentioned that maybe he should be on "city highballs" today too, like I was yesterday. I said, "Won't we look good, walking into a saloon and both ordering a glass of water."

That reminded me of when Buddy went into Hartung's one time and didn't order right away. Ike, the bartender, would greet you with, "What did you come in for, to get warm?"

Since we were close to our old neighborhood, I thought it might be a good idea to drive through and see how things look. Coming to Buddy's old house we first noticed the front door with its leaded panels. His grandma was so proud of the lovely door. The house looked in pretty good shape. However, my old house didn't appear as if anyone was living in it. The wood siding that my dad was so proud of had been stripped away. It looked kind of like a skinned cat. My dad always made sure that Mr. Keehan, the painter, kept the house looking nice. Thus, he had him paint it every several years. Maybe that's the reason the siding had been stripped away. He always used lead paint. (Today it is such a big deal about how lead paint now affects you. Of course, my dad didn't know about that so he didn't think that way.)

Each year, before the summer began, he got a gallon of white lead paint with the little "Dutch Boy" on it, added a little linseed oil, and my brother and I would spend a day painting away. Oh, it made that old porch so smooth and on hot summer nights we would lay on it instead of going to bed. My mom always said we were kind of crazy, especially when I came home and told her I had joined the Army. Her remark was, "I always thought there was something wrong with your mind."

So, now I know the reason, lead paint! As we looked around the old neighborhood, we reminisced about all the old neighbors: the Kings, the Moores, old Mary Stone, the Massaris, etc., all of whom have passed on. In those days, you knew who lived in houses for blocks around. Buddy said, "Today we don't even know who lives next door to us. If it were not for names on the mailboxes in my Florida condo, I wouldn't know my next door neighbor."

As we made our way up Elberon Avenue, we noted that Mr. Keehan's Paint Shop is now a recycling place. The sign says, they take aluminum, copper, and even gold. Maybe they got started with the aluminum cans they found hidden throughout the place left by the painters. Hoagy, one of the painters, always said it was good to start off the day with a few beers. He said that would give you a steady hand and make it easier to climb those ladders. "Yeah, that's where he got started," Buddy remembered. "Then he went on to becoming a business agent for all the painters."

Mt. Echo Tavern ◊ Bohemian ◊ Mary's House: "Buddy, look at the old Mt. Echo Tavern all boarded up. Red's dad, Mr. Jaspers, would not like to see that. He always kept the place so nice. Red and Bob also did a good job after their dad passed away. It was probably one of the best saloons on the Hill. Next door to where Mr. Wessel was running his electrical business was Mr. Pierson's drycleaning business. Mr. Wessel's dad ran the Bohemian, the one that was next to St. Lawrence Church. You know, there were two of them on the Hill? I guess, if the electric business got bad, he could move next door and open Red's old place. Mary's House used to be on the corner. The house is gone and has been replaced by a convenience store; there's plenty of them around the Hill. It seems they have taken the place of the mom-and-pop stores we once knew."

"Buddy, speaking of mom-and-pop stores, there was Mr. Comer's Grocery. He sure sold a lot of beer. Those women who liked to have a few drinks in the afternoon and not let their neighbors know would have the beer delivered with the groceries. A fellow stopped at the Price Hill Historical Society & Museum several months ago. He went to West High and told us he would not have gotten through high school if it wasn't for Mr. Comer. Every morning before going to school, he would go through Dempsey Park. He always knew he could find a few quart beer bottles there. He would then take them over to Comer's and cash them in. He would get a doughnut and a bottle of milk; then he was off to school to do his lessons."

Gus Wagner's/Lee's Café: Gus Wagner's/Lee's Café has been turned into a coffeehouse. That seems to be the modern thing today. I guess Harry and Jack would rather see it that way than what has happened to other saloons. "Let's go in and take a look. I've never been to a coffeehouse before. What does that sign say? Two bucks for a cup of coffee! We could go up the street to White Castle for half that price."

We notice that the old icehouse that sat across the street is gone. That used to be our meeting place when the Gym closed for the summer. "Buddy, remember when we sat there, the police would not run us off! But, if we stood on the corner, that old cop by the name of Allen was always on us. He ran all the St. Teresa's guys in one night. Father Anthony went down to the jail and bailed them out. The next week old Allen was walking a beat in the West End."

On hot summer nights, Big Herm would come from across the street and open the icebox door to get some ice. That cold air would come out of the box and you would feel like you were in heaven. In those days, some real characters hung out in the saloons. Old Pete and Lou, who would dig foundations for houses, using a pick and shovel. Boy, how they could work! But best of all was Champ's Uncle Lou, who would come over and talk with us. He had all kinds of stories about how he rode a motorcycle. But best of all was the story about the greyhound he bet on at the dog track in Harrison, who won by a tail. He told us how the dogs all caught the rabbit at the finish line. As the dogs were all fighting over the rabbit, his big red dog was real timid and didn't want to get in the fight. In backing away from the scrimmage, he backed over the finish line and was declared the winner. Oh, what a story!

I was just remembering a day when Elder got out for summer vacation. We were all sitting on the icehouse thinking what we were going to do all summer. Lou came out of the saloon with some guy. He was going to show him that Model-A Ford, of which he was so proud. We didn't know that Yake had put an auto bomb on it. He turned on the key, that auto bomb went off and smoke poured out from under the hood. His friend took off running because he thought for sure that the Mafia was after Lou. Yake was laughing so hard, he was almost rolling in the street. Lou saw this and knew who had done it. He took off running after Yake. If he would have caught him, he would have killed him. Good for Yake, he was the fastest guy around. Oh Boy! What a start to that summer!

Dittleberger ◊ *Welz Tavern:* Heading up Hawthorne Avenue to Warsaw Avenue, we saw that Dugan's Drugstore was gone. It is now replaced by a chili parlor. Pretty soon that's all there'll be on the Hill. We are now looking at a "For Sale" sign on the last saloon on Warsaw Avenue, Dittleberger's. Years ago it was Welz Tavern. Today it too has a big lock on the door. We saw someone coming out of the locked building and we approached him. He told us that he used to be a part-time bartender and a porter. As we looked inside we could see that the only thing left in the bar was where the bartender used to draw up the beers. All the tables and chairs were missing. It was hard to understand how one could sell a business with all the essentials gone. As we asked him what happened to all the business they once had, he told us a story which seems to be prevalent in the saloon business today, "No Smoking!" Then he added, "How can you tell a bunch of 'hardy drinkers' who hang in your saloon that they're not allowed to smoke?" He said it got so bad that the health inspector was more interested in seeing if there were any cigarette butts on the floor than how clean the place was.

Just think of all the years that Carrie Nation worked so hard to shut down saloons in Cincinnati. The state legislators have

122

accomplished this by signing a bill forbidding smoking inside of buildings. It's hard to imagine that you're not allowed to smoke at a baseball or football stadium. (Thinking about bringing a casino to Cincinnati with no smoking allowed, just doesn't seem to be a good bet. Can you imagine someone playing a slot machine and having to go outside when they feel a need to smoke? Maybe they'll have little signs to put on the slot machines, "Player gone to smoke, do not use this machine.")

While outside Dittleberger's old saloon building, we thought back when in a shorter distance than from home plate to first base, one could count three saloons, all of them doing a good business. In the heyday of saloons along Warsaw Avenue from here out to Quebec Road, there were some fifteen establishments that sold beer and liquor. That doesn't even include the numerous grocery stores that also sold beer.

"Buddy, I thought for sure we would hear some music by Doris Day coming from the apartment windows upstairs. The music one might hear today is quite a change from that time. Speaking of Doris Day, do you remember when we were too young to drink and would stop by Welz Tavern to get a barbecue sandwich for fifteen cents? That was one of the best buys around, and to think that you were served by someone who was soon to become a famous movie star!"

Well, it's going to be pretty dry as we make our way out the Pike. We used to only walk four or five blocks and by hitting each saloon along the way, we would be pretty well loaded. The old library, along this stretch just celebrated its one-hundredth birthday. We reminisced how the guys in the neighborhood used to play football on the nice, green lawn at the Price Hill Library. They would swing on the flagpole rope like they were Tarzan.

Buddy said, "Yeah, I can remember when Angie swung on the pole. He was so heavy, the pole bent, and everyone took off."

"Speaking of Angie, his dad ran an Italian store across the street. When you walked in there it smelled of garlic so bad that it took you a week to get the smell off your clothes. Then, right next to that store, was an Italian barber. That block was like the 'Little Italy' of Price Hill."

White Castle has taken over where Strassburger's Bakery once was. I can remember the coupons that used to be in the Sunday paper that let you get five hamburgers for a quarter. I think now they are about a buck apiece. Of course, in those days we used to say they did not have any meat on them. They were nothing but onions and pickles and one could eat them on Fridays.

Speaking of the bakery, I remember how you could get a dozen filled doughnuts for thirty cents. The kids were always told not to drop the bag on their feet. The donuts were so heavy they would break your toe, and Ida would always throw in an apple turnover or a cream roll. Now one donut costs twice as much as a dozen did in those days.

"What is that new building were the Price Hill Roller Rink once was?"

"That's the new Salvation Army building. Boy, they sure must have collected a lot of nickels to build that. Remember how those ladies wearing their uniforms would hit all the saloons with their tambourines a jingling?"

"Yeah Froggy, and we would sing that little parody, "Put a nickel in the drum, save another drunken bum, Hallelujah!"

"But they do a lot of good work with the kids in the neighborhood and with their after-school programs."

It looks like some guy fixes violins in what was once Mother Stone's Chili Parlor. She had that one pinball machine, I guess it helped to pay the rent. Mike was always trying to beat the machine, using that little "special nickel" he had. It was a half nickel on a wire. As usual, they ran him out of a lot of places when they caught him using it.

Krogers cleaned out several blocks when they built their new store. Along with Huber's Department Store and several saloons, the grocery chain came in and took over. The old Provident Bank across the street is where I had my first Christmas savings. Boy, I thought I was rich when I got the $12.50 shortly before Christmas. I was ready to buy everyone a present. Most of my shopping was down the street at the five-and-dime store. That bank building is now the Price Hill Historical Society and Museum.

The Price Hill Historical Society and Museum, formerly a Provident Bank branch office, on Warsaw Avenue

"Buddy, before you head back down south, you have to come in for a visit. It will bring back a lot of memories of your days on the Hill. In fact I think I saw a few pictures of you in your baseball uniform. The Price Hill Historical Society has plans for a room dedicated to nothing but sports memorabilia on their second floor. Harry Lee and Mike Kunnen are always showing up with old-time pictures. Mike is still running the Old-Time Ballplayers' Banquet each May."

Then Buddy said, "I sure did like to go to those banquets when I was living up here. You got a chance to meet some of the best ballplayers on the Hill. What's that building across the way that has "Price Hill Will" on it?"

"It used to be old Doc Lampe's building and the Price Hill Will is a group trying to bring back some of the old charm that was once Price Hill. They've bought up many buildings and homes and rehabbed them. Along with that, they provide various projects and programs like "Holiday on the Hill" in December. They are really doing a good job."

"Speaking of old Doc Lampe, remember how for years he was Elder's doctor? I can remember old Dren getting hurt in a game on a Sunday and Bart would send him down to Doc early Monday morning. He would tape him up and tell him he'd be okay to play by the end of the week. You just don't get doctors who are that devoted today."

I told Buddy that after Doc Lampe gave up his practice, Doctor Finke took over. He was in that building for almost fifty years before retiring. In fact, when he quit, he gave all his equipment and furnishings to the Price Hill Historical Society and Museum. Along with Dr. Finke's and Dr. Beekley's office equipment, the Society really has some antiques. Dr. Beekley's office was located on Warsaw Avenue, next to the District 3 police station.

We are now heading over Cemetery Street to Eighth Street, and maybe we can get a drink over there. You might be thinking that I meant to say Enright Avenue and not Cemetery Street. However, before the bridge on Eighth Street was built over Woodlawn and Fairbanks Avenues, funeral processions coming to the Hill had to use Warsaw Avenue. Then they would cut over, thus the name Cemetery Street. Speaking of the Eighth Street Bridge, it had that little railing, which was about two inches wide on the top. Yake would get on one side and Georgie on the other and they would walk across the rail to see who could get to the other side the fastest. Norm would be wringing his hands, thinking for sure one was going to fall off down to Fairbanks. They could drop down a couple hundred feet to the street below and someone would have to pick them up with a blotter. It never happened; they always made it. And Yake was fast, but Georgie was always was the fastest.

There's nothing left of the old icehouse that was at Price and Enright. I remember how in the summer, the old trucks with those solid rubber tires would haul that ice, day and night, down Elberon Avenue. If we were having a hayride, we always knew we could stop the ice truck. Mickey would ice our beer for us. He would just say, "Have a good time, the ice is on me!"

Paradise Lounge ◊ Lyon's Den ◊ Mause's Saloon: As we pulled to the curb along Enright Avenue and West Eighth Street, my friend looked at the palm trees and flamingos on the side of what use to be the Lyon's Den. He thought he was back in Florida. The sign said it was now the Paradise Lounge. As we entered,

126

we thought for sure we would run into Jimmy Buffet, all dressed up in his Key West clothing with a parrot on his shoulder, or his head. My friend was pretty dry by this time and needed a beer. Lori, the barmaid, was quick to be of service. She was all ears as we told her about how at one time, this was Mause's Saloon. We told her that after a burial across the street, the family usually came here to drown their sorrows. The Irish were buried on one side of the street and the Germans on the other. It was news to her that the cemeteries on either side of the street were reserved for different ethnic groups.

My friend noted that years ago, when he was in the bar, this was one of the longest bars in Price Hill. It seemed much shorter today. Also, part of the back bar was missing. I already mentioned the story about the bar at the Lyon's Den earlier in the book. The bar, along with the back bar, were taken out of the Lyon's Den by a guy for his basement bar and then later purchased by the owners of Market Street Grill in Harrison. So now what was originally part of Mause's Bar, one of the oldest in Price Hill, has a history in Harrison, Ohio. It kind of goes with what we are seeing happening around the Hill today. Many of Price Hill descendants have moved out further west to places like Harrison and Bright, Indiana, too.

As I was getting ready to leave, I asked Lori if she ever heard any strange sounds, like fire bells ringing. She replied that she heard bells in the distance but thought those might be church bells. I had to tell her that probably Georgie, an old-time firefighter, was ringing a bell at one end of the bar. He would ring the bell to try and awaken Marshal Bob at the other end of the bar, to get him to go to a fire. Maybe he would do that in order to kid him about the buildings he burnt down, that are now parking lots. However, this didn't faze Marshal Bob too much.

Jimmy used to tell the tale about Bob's wife lugging two big bags of groceries from the nearby Kroger. Bob told her to put them in the car and he would bring them home later. As she walked out the door, Jimmy said, "Aren't you going to give her a ride home?" Bob told him no, because the walk would do her good and he had two beers on base. Jimmy just went on tending bar and shaking his head. Georgie, from the other end of the bar, commented, "At least he let her put the groceries in the car. It was surprising that he didn't make her carry them home." Oh well, it takes all kinds to hang in saloons.

Cottage Tavern ◊ *Sunset Lounge:* We moved on and made our way out West Eighth Street to what used to be the Cottage Tavern. Since those days it has had quite a few different names, but the Sunset Lounge seems to have lasted the longest. We noticed the door was locked, even though it was mid-afternoon, so we decided to go to Terry's barber shop, Grote Barber Styling, and see what was going on. Terry Grote was waiting for a customer, so we sat and talked for a spell. Since he is a member of the Business Association, he knows about all the businesses on the Hill. He told us that the Sunset Lounge doesn't open until around six and the crowd is mostly a young group.

There always was a problem with parking on West Eighth Street with its no parking zone from four to six o'clock. There is nothing worse than to have one of your customers get a parking ticket or to have their car towed—you'll never see them again. The police today must go to school for speed-writing. As soon as someone hollers, "They're ticketing your car!" you run out and the officer says, "Sorry, got the ticket written already."

That was not the case when Poots Poland would patrol the streets of Price Hill on his three-wheeler. Before he would write a ticket, he would go into the business and ask if the car out front of the place belonged to someone in the place. He knew merchants had a hard time getting customers and he wasn't going to drive them away. It isn't any wonder that he was one of the best-liked cops on the Hill.

Buddy curiously asked, "By the way, do you see him anymore?"

"I usually see him a couple of times each week visiting his wife."

"Is she in a home?"

"No, she is in a permanent home in the cemetery at the end of the car line and he never misses a day of visiting her grave."

128

"Well Buddy, if you don't need a haircut, you can go next door and Terry's wife in the beauty shop can get rid of some of that grey hair with some of the dye she has. Your wife won't know you when I take you home today."

"I doubt that, because her old saying is that the snow might be on the roof but still there's no fire in the stove."

Trenton Tavern: Since we were on West Eighth Street, we headed up the street to the Trenton Tavern. The place doesn't look much different from when Tubby had it. The old beer case that looks like a giant milk bottle is still there, but the booths look like they could use a good overhaul. The last time I was in here was years ago on a Sunday just before Christmas. Tubby owned the place and, like many saloons on the Hill at that time, they threw a Christmas party for all their customers. I can remember the table in the back room being loaded with food. It mostly had been made by Dolly, Tubby's wife. Hot roast beef, ham, and even deviled eggs; it kind of reminded you of the days before Prohibition when they would provide free lunch for the customers. I guess you'll never see that again.

From Trenton Tavern we went over to Sunset Avenue and back to Glenway Avenue. On Sunset we marveled how good the old St. William School looked. I told Buddy about the bingos they used to have there. They were the first to have a top prize of one thousand dollars. The streetcars used to line up four or five deep to take the players home. They came from all over the city. We talked about having a thousand dollars in those days as being a lot of money. Today they talk in "millions." I had just recently heard that someone from Kentucky had won the lottery and it was something like $120 million. We agreed that we wouldn't know what to do with that kind of money.

Looking at St. William's new gym behind the school brought back memories of that old one they had. It actually had several posts right out on the floor. When you played the guys from St. William, they knew how to dribble around the posts. We would always run into the posts trying to dribble down the floor. No wonder that the guys like Lenny and Duke from St. William were so good.

"Some of these old houses around here are really in good shape. They call this area Cedar Grove, which was the original name of the grounds around Seton High School; it was named by the nuns that owned it."

"Our friend Yake's old house still looks pretty good and that wall he rebuilt still looks good, too."

"You know Buddy, several years ago we had quite a few hard rains and a section of it fell down. I was glad to see it returned to its original shape by the current owners. Otherwise, Yake would have been looking down from above, worrying about it. Knowing him, he might have even asked the Lord if he could have a little time off because of a job he needed to finish."

"Buddy, just look at Elder's football field (The Pit); how nice and green it is. That's not grass; several years ago they put down Astroturf. Wonder if they covered up that sewer lid that used to be on the forty yard line? It was always nice to set someone up for a tackle right on top of it. The next time they'd know better and would take a different route."

"Hey Froggy, what are all those decks behind those houses on Regina?"

"A bunch of guys went together and they bought one of those old houses and fixed it up. They made a pavilion out in the back

The view of "The Pit" from a deck on Regina Avenue

One of the decks on Regina Avenue built to overlook Elder's "Pit"

looking over the field. They kind of remind me of the houses over the wall at Wrigley Field in Chicago. They have about ten or twelve guys in the club and they grill and sit up there with a beer and watch the game. This concept spread over to several more houses behind the press box. However, they had to elevate their decks to get a view over the press box. "

"You know "The Pit" has got a pretty good reputation," I told Buddy. "It was rated as one of the ten best places in the country to watch a high school game. Just this past season, on the first Sunday in September, they televised a game across the country."

"Yeah, you know I was having lunch with some guys in a bar down in Florida and all of a sudden, I looked up and saw these kids in purple running out onto the field. These guys just couldn't believe that I had gone to that school."

"You know Buddy, that televised Elder game reminded me of one of the Thanksgiving games years ago. The streets were filled with people going to the game. Guys were tailgating all over the place. In fact, some people from Colerain were tailgating in front of my house and you know I live about a half mile from the Pit.

Elder won that game, but they lost to Moeller and St. Xavier. But, in the end they got even and beat St. X in the playoffs and went clear to the State Finals."

On our drive over to Elder I remembered the old Albers store that was where the school's front parking lot is today. "Buddy, just think, when we went to Elder, there were only about ten cars in the student parking lot, most from the Bridgetown, Cheviot, or Delhi guys who drove. Hal, with the back of his car bashed in, was the only one from Holy Family. Most guys would hit a pole with the front of the car; he is the only one I ever knew to slide backwards into a pole. Look, Seton didn't build a parking lot, they built a multistory garage. Someone once said that S. C. doesn't mean Sisters of Charity; it really means Sisters of Commerce. They always did know how to get the best for their buck."

We walked over and looked at the plaque they put up for Bart (Walter Bartlett) at Elder's "Pit." They named the field after him in 2009. Father Bertke said the prayer during the ceremony. I guess that was the last official act he had at his favorite place, as he died December 1, 2009.

He was around there at Elder for a long time. I remember his first year teaching American History. The textbook for that class was about as thick as a telephone book and he thought nothing of throwing it at you if he caught you sleeping in class.

Buddy remarked, "Yeah, I know all about that thick

Father Erwin Bertke and Walter "Babe" Bartlett, from the 1947 Elderado yearbook from Elder High School

132

Fr. Bertke, third from left, at the dedication of Walter Bartlett Field at Elder in 2009

book. I went home with a few headaches. It's nice that they have the plaque in this location, since this was Bart's favorite place to scrimmage before they built the fieldhouse. He loved to let Hunchy run over us freshmen to get him ready for a game on the weekend. When practice was over, you felt like you'd been run over by a train."

Today there are no more worries about a place to scrimmage. The school has an area they call the PAC down off Quebec Road. Some alumni guys raised money and bought the land. Elder now has all kinds of fields down there. I told Buddy that if we had some time we would go and take a look.

After our visit to Elder, we got back on Glenway Avenue. I pointed out that what use to be Hoinke's Bowling Alleys is now a Family Dollar store. It seems like I see them all over. They took over for what used to be the five-and-dime stores. Boy, I remembered watching some good bowlers up there, probably some of the best in the country. There were a few from around here that could hold their own with anyone. Just like every other thing, Hoinke had to grow and moved further out of Price Hill.

The 52 Bar: We saw the 52 Bar sign. Buddy Asked, "Didn't that used be down on Warsaw Avenue?"

"Yeah, but they moved out here, and did you notice that they added 'Tim' to the '52' and that the sign is purple? I guess that's what you do when you're right across from Elder."

"Buddy, I know you must be pretty dry; let's go in so you can have a cold one. Too bad the owner's not here. I always wanted to know how the 52 came about, because neither the former nor present location has a 52 in their address. I once heard a rumor that years ago, when they got their license, they were the fifty-second bar on Price Hill. I have this old picture of Bender's Tavern that was right next door; I'm going to show the barmaid."

The barmaid was not aware that Bender's was one of the first saloons on the Hill and that the territory around here was originally known as the Village of Warsaw. Recently they tore the old building next door down and, as is the case in most saloons today, they kind of use the area for an outdoor beer garden so the smokers have a place to light-up.

"Buddy, there are some big bruisers here with those Bengal shirts on, so don't be telling them you are a Dolphin fan or we'll have to fight our way out of here. I know you did that a few times, but you were a lot younger and it's hard to count the number of times you went out the door with a bloody nose. So keep quiet, drink your beer, and I'll drink my water, and we will be on our way. I'm sure glad it isn't a Sunday with the Bengals playing Miami. I know for sure you would have mouthed off about how good the Dolphins are and how lousy the Bengals are. One of those guys wearing those Bengal shirts would have thrown both of us out the front door."

As we motored on out Glenway Avenue, we noticed all the buildings that are now torn down that formerly housed saloons, along with other businesses. It seems that City Hall loves to tear down buildings. Right across the street from Radel Funeral Home was an apartment building. It was a problem to the police and the way they solved the problem was to tear down a whole block. Yes, even the old Eagles Hall is now gone.

"Buddy, we sure had some good Saturday nights there. You could bring your own bottle and drink 'n' drown. Some nights, when we walked out of there, we really were drowned. Kind of reminds me of that commercial with a guy driving a car full of beer; the police officer stops him, opens the door, and it just pours out. He asks, "Have you been drinking?"

French Villa: We remembered the old French Villa. You could always get a date there on a Saturday night. All the nursing students from Dunham Hospital would hang out there. You could take them to a show at the Glenway or the Western Plaza Theaters for only a quarter and then have a beer afterwards, knowing they had to be back by ten. When the Sunset Theater opened, things got a little more expensive. It cost thirty-five cents, but they had those double aisle seats where you and your date could be real close and sit in one seat. The property of French Villa was eventually purchased by Glenway Chevrolet. The Sunset Theater, on the opposite corner of the French Villa property, was taken over by the Knights of Columbus Hall and then was bought by Glenway Chevrolet.

In recent years, Glenway Chevrolet moved their operations out to Ferguson and Glenhills Way, leaving the Glenway and Sunset Avenue site empty and available. Awhile back, General Motors shut down Glenway Chevrolet along with a bunch of dealers after the government bailed them out. It's so sad to see a ninety-year-old business being forced to close their operation.

The empty Glenway Chevrolet dealership building was purchased by Cincinnati Public Schools for a new Carson School. The old Carson School with the big clock tower was torn down. They just tore everything down and threw it away. I went up one day and looked in the dumpster. They were throwing away desks that were better than what most parochial schools are using today. The more I look at that new Carson School, the more I notice all the different colors of brick. It looks like a factory that is advertising the different types of bricks they handle.

I told Buddy how I remember some of our desks having so many initials carved in them that it was difficult to write on them. Harry was a classmate who got a knife for Christmas one year. When we got back to school, he would carve his initials in every desk he sat in. He wasn't too bright, because there was only one kid in the class with the initials H. N. I can remember Sister grabbing him by the ear and marching him to the office. For the next month of Saturdays he did nothing but sand desks. In those days, nuns sure knew how to twist ears.

On our continuing excursion, I pointed out that the old Sears store on Glenway Avenue is another one of those Dollar Stores. My mom and dad used to do all their shopping there, dad for his tools and mom for all of our clothes.

In this same area, Russ Brogan's auto service has still survived. Russ will also fill you in on all that is happening around Elder. I told Buddy that if he needed a new pair of tires before heading back south, he had better stop and see Russ. Across the street, his brother Dave can fix you up with a tux if you're planning on celebrating the new year in style. And their Elder sons are continuing their family businesses.

Hartung's Café: Well, I guess Bob Hartung is looking down on his old saloon from up above. Seeing today's snow piled up on the sidewalk reminded me of Bob's favorite saying, "I did not put it there and I am not going to take it away." His poor old customers would try and make their way down the steps without slipping and breaking their jug of beer, sometimes unsuccessfully. As Louis from the gas station on the other corner used to say, "Hartung could write a book on how not to run a business."

Standing on the corner and looking to the west and reminiscing, we could see some of the finest businesses on the Hill. Evangeline Candy made some of the best chocolates. Then there was Wolff's Drug Store. If you were feeling bad or had a cold, no need to go to the doctor. Just tell him your symptoms and they would fix you up with something. And, across the street, one wonders how two butcher shops, Pop Roell and Mr. Fussner's Meats, could survive so close to each other. A tragedy also comes to mind. This neighborhood was in total shock when the "Cin-

136

cinnati Strangler" came here and killed a lady in her basement on Rutledge Avenue. I also remember when things got really busy on the streetcar line; the Warsaw car took the short route and turned at the "Carson Loop." This location became a United Dairy Farmer store, giving way later to yet another convenient store.

I noticed as we passed by the firehouse that the statue of their Dalmatian dog has purple spots rather than the usual black spots. I guess there must be some Elder alumni stationed there. I also saw that the bench is painted purple and white; on game days, if you drive by, you might see a bed sheet hanging from the second floor window with "Go Elder" painted on it. I noticed several young ladies in front of the house. They obviously have lady firefighters now. In fact, the city has about thirty-five or forty lady firefighters. In my day, any wife would really have liked one saying they had slept in the bedroom with a few young ladies. Her remarks would have been, "Start looking for a new job because the only lady to sleep in your bedroom is me!"

Turning south at Rapid Run Road, we soon came to the corner that was the turnaround hole for the Elberon Country Club. The old clubhouse is still standing up on Overlook Avenue; it is a church today.

I have already mentioned that there is a lot of history in this area. At the corner of Hermosa and St. Lawrence Avenues, gates used to lead into George Remus' estate. Those gates have since made their way to Elder at Regina and Vincent Avenues. As many times as we passed through those gates, little did we know about their history.

Passing West Eighth Street and Pedretti Avenue brings back many memories of catching the bus on a Sunday night in the summer and heading out to either Green's Woods or Lauterbach's Grove for a picnic. Buddy said that I forgot to mention the Mt. Alverno Festival. "Remember how the brothers used to bake that rye bread and serve ham sandwiches? What was better than sitting under the tent eating a sandwich and having a beer?" I reminded Buddy about old Pete with his squeeze box and how we would all join in singing songs.

137

The Elberon streetcar, perhaps the very one commandeered by Froggy and Yake

I will never forget the night we all took the bus back up here and the Elberon streetcar was sitting up by the cemetery at the end of the line. So we all walked up and got on. The motorman must have been in the Crow's Nest. The next thing we knew, our friend Yake had gotten at the controls and the streetcar was headed down West Eighth Street. He acted like a real motorman and even stopped by St. William Church to pick up a passenger. The guy showed his pass and took a seat. When we got to West Eighth Street and Elberon Avenue, Yake stopped the car and we all bailed out like a bunch of rats, abandoning ship and taking off running. To this day, I wonder how that motorman explained to his supervisor how he lost his streetcar. I still can remember the look on our passenger's face, wondering what the heck was going on.

"Froggy, speaking of streetcars I see you have several pictures of old cars laying here on the seat. Where did you get them?"

"Buddy, Phil Lind brought them to the Price Hill Historical Society. He is a streetcar buff; I think he has a picture of every streetcar that ever ran in the city. Did you notice that these pictures were all taken with saloons in the background? But I'll bet you he doesn't have any with someone hanging on the back, especially on that Elberon car. Remember it had a little ledge you could put your feet on and hold onto the sign? I remember how a car would go up Elberon and there would be two or three guys from Eighth and State hanging on the back. I don't think they knew what the inside of a streetcar looked like. Instead of ringing the bell to get off at their stop, they would just pull the rope and the trolley would come off the wire and they would jump off. Those motormen hated when they had to get out and put the trolleys back on the wire. I saw something in the paper recently, where they wanted to bring streetcars back in the Over the Rhine area. It will be interesting to see if the kids can ride on the back of the new streetcars. I guess they'll probably have a police car following every trolley."

The Blue Note: "The Blue Note over there looks like it got a lot bigger than when we knew it. They've got sand volleyball courts and the like. Remember the jam sessions on a Sunday afternoon? We were packed in so tight that there was no chance anyone could start a fight. Half the time you couldn't raise your arms to drink your beer, much less swing a punch. Norma, the owner, was smart; she usually picked the biggest guy in the place to be the unofficial bouncer. She gave him free beer all afternoon and there was never any trouble. Some Sundays, we came out of there feeling no pain. I remember the day Olk, one of the guys that hung out at The Blue Note, got his pilots license and he was going to take all of us up in an airplane. We got out to Lunken Airport and he couldn't get the hanger door open. I guess we were real lucky. With the condition he was in, we would have probably landed in some tree tops over in Fort Thomas, KY."

Curnayn's ◊ Doll's Saloon: "Over the years, Curnayn's has not changed much. Buddy, you know that right next door, where the beauty shop is, was a saloon called Doll's. It was probably one of the first saloons in this area, even before the Crow's Nest. In fact, one of the streets around here was named Doll Street, before they started to change names of streets."

"The last time I was in Curnayn's was when we used to all go in on Saturdays after golfing at the Dunham course. Still have a cap with 'Hendley Invitational' on it. I was wearing it in Florida when I was playing golf. Some guy asked me how big that invitational was. I told him 'real big!' I was not about to tell him it was played on a nine-hole course. He would've laughed at me. I could have told him 'Daddy Rabbit' won the tournament and then he really would've gone wild. Remember our old friend Daddy showing up with his knickers on? You would think he was the best golfer in the city. He was lucky if he could get the ball close to the green on a nine-hole course. Yeah, and then he would come back to the saloon and talk about the game he had. We really had some good times on a Saturday morning."

"I guess all those guys are gone. Wonder if any of the Hilltoppers Club (a social club in Price Hill) is still around? They were really generous at this time of year, primarily at Christmas, passing out food baskets to needy families."

Jack and Jill's: As we looked at where Jack and Jill's used to be, I remembered the horseshoe courts they had in the backyard. I used to like to come up there and watch the guys pitch. If you couldn't throw a ringer with every shoe, you better not get in the game. It seemed like every time you looked, there would be four shoes stacked on top of each other on the peg. There aren't any players like that around today. All you see are guys playing cornhole. "So, Buddy, has cornhole hit Florida yet? Up here they have tournaments and if you're really good, you can win yourself some money."

Crow's Nest: I told Buddy that I sure was glad to see that the Crow's Nest has a new sign. I told him that I would never forget that piece of plywood with the name on it that Big Jim, the fireman who had bought the Crow's Nest, put up. I told him how one night about ten o'clock, Spade, our painter friend, came along with some of his ladders and Big Jim had us hang that sign. Someone asked him why we couldn't do it during the daytime and his reply was, "The building inspector will see us and I'll have to get a permit." Big Jim was always holding court at the end of the bar, with that big cigar in his mouth!

"A lot of firemen said farewell to the department with their retirement party on the second floor of the Crow's Nest. Now it is owned by Glen O'Dell and his wife. Let's stop in and see them."

I noticed that the sign in the window says, "Best Fish Sandwich in Town."

"Yeah, several years ago during Lent, the Enquirer had a contest as to who had the best fish sandwich in town and they were voted the best. Their sandwich is codfish and you really get a big portion."

The O'Dell's also have a chili parlor further out on Glenway Avenue. Their chili is a little different than Skyline's. It is something more like your mom used to make every Saturday night. She would throw the beans, spaghetti, and the like all into the pot. Boy, I really liked that! Drink up, Buddy, we are going to head over to Clearview Lake."

Clearview Lake: "Up here, the popular fish today is catfish. I can't get it too much. All I can think of are the ones we used to catch at Clearview Lake. You'd pull them out and they had those big whiskers that looked like cat's whiskers."

"By the way, Froggy, I had been by Clearview Lake earlier and I noticed the pond is still there, but the building has been torn down."

"Well, Don, the owner, got pretty sick and was going to sell the business. Delhi came along and gave him about a half million bucks to expand the park, so they tore down the building. One thing you could say about Don, he was one of the shrewdest saloon operators."

We doubled back to Overlook and passed by St. Teresa School; the gym brought back memories of growing up in the 1940s. This gym was one of the finest in the city for a grade school. I reminded Buddy how much fun it was to play a game of basketball there, with all the wide open spaces. I remembered the dances on Sunday nights they would have for us high school kids. All the boys would be lined up against the wall, talking, and the girls would be dancing together. Father Anthony would say, "Why are you guys not out there dancing?" Never will forget the night that one of our friends, Big Murph, blew on Father's bald head. He turned around and said, "Is that what they teach you at Elder?"

It seems that Murph always had a little problem with guys' heads. I'll never forget the night he put his hand on a guy's head and said, "Boy, you really got a head of hair!" Next thing he knew he had the guy's toupee in his hand. He didn't know whether to put it back on his head or put it in his pocket. We all got a big laugh out of that. I sure did feel sorry for the bald-headed guy.

Old Time Saloon/Ideal Café: "What is the "Old Time Saloon" all about? The only thing I ever knew it by was the Ideal. After the 11:30 a.m. mass at St. Teresa, it would look like they were having Benediction at the Ideal. The last time I was here was for a gin rummy game one afternoon. Boy, did I get my clock cleaned that day. Penny-a-point doesn't sound like much, but when you were playing with those pros, one could go broke in a hurry. Moon and Tommie were a couple of those guys. Moon would sit on that chair on his haunches and after you picked up one discard, he could tell you every card in your hand, just like he had x-ray eyes. And Tommie was even better. He lived and died playing gin."

"Buddy, someone told me that he and his wife went along with several other couples to Myrtle Beach. Tommie played gin and drank beer the whole time. I don't think he ever looked at the ocean once. I guess that bunch has all passed on. For years they made the rounds of the Ideal, Hartung's, and the Crow's Nest. If you stopped in those places in the afternoon, for sure you could see a game of cards being played. I guess with all of today's casinos, very seldom do you see any card games in saloons."

We talked about Prout's Corner and how it has changed. The old Overlook Show is gone. Us guys from the ghetto did not get out that far too often. Usually either the Plaza or the Glenway Theater had the same movies. The Kroger at Prout's Corner is gone, along with the ten cent store, but Hart's Drug Store keeps on going. I told Buddy how those big chain drug stores don't seem to faze the Hart family at all.

"Remember the fun we used to have bowling at Overlook Lanes? We really thought we were in a big bowling alley with six lanes, after coming from the Gym with only two."

"Yeah, and they also had four pool tables."

"I think we best skip the Golden Fleece tonight, Buddy. I am afraid you will get in there, run into a bunch of Elder boys and I will have to deposit you on the porch again, ring the bell, and take off running."

"Yeah, that's okay. Me and the wife had breakfast there this past Wednesday morning and who was in there but Rube, Bob, and Al, with their wives. They call themselves the Pilgrims. They go to Mass at St. Lawrence and then come to Sam's Price Hill Chili for breakfast. My wife was in heaven. Not only did she get her goetta, but got to meet a bunch of old girlfriends she had not seen in years. I noticed that a bunch of old Elder boys were meeting there, but also some old-timers from West Hi. My wife could eat goetta every morning while we are here; nothing like that in Florida. Then at night, it's out to get a three-way. You know, the other night we went out for dinner and after dinner I asked her if she would like an after dinner drink, a crème de menthe or a Drambuie, and she said no. 'I'll settle for a Graeter's cone,' was her request. So, there we were sitting at Graeter's eating a raspberry chocolate chip cone. Boy, how things have changed!"

"Buddy, have you noticed that Price Hill Chili has now added a garden and fishpond outside? Maybe Sam could throw a few jack salmon in there and add that to the menu. You know, it's hard to find them anymore. It used to be that every bar serving fish would have them on the menu. None was any better than those you used to get at Schulte's down at Anderson Ferry on River Road. Remember how we used to bum a streetcar pass on Sunday night and go down there? We would get a jack salmon fish sandwich and a bag of french fries, sit down by the railroad tracks and watch the trains go by. We thought we were in heaven. Remember how we would look in that back window at Schulte's where they were frying the fish and those big kettles of grease would be boiling? They would throw the fish in the kettle and in a matter of several minutes they came out good and brown. I think every kid that lived in Riverside got their start working in that kitchen. The added fun was riding on that old Fernbank streetcar. It was like a ride on one of the roller coasters at Coney."

"It is so nice to see the Covedale Theater and the old United Savings building as the Covedale Library. How did Price Hill ever manage to save those two icons?"

"Well, Buddy, after they sat vacant for awhile, they wanted to tear them down and make them into a Burger King. The Civic Club got busy and got some people interested in them and they were preserved. It sure does make a difference in the area. Remember the old library as a little store building up the street? The theater really puts on some good plays and attracts a lot of people to the Hill. Boy, that old theater was the Cadillac of movie houses during its time. About a week after the good shows were downtown, they would be on the screen up here. Taking your date there would really feel like a great night out."

J & J ◊ Corner Pub/Caritas: "Is the old J & J, on Glenway and Ferguson, another coffeehouse? Jack, the bartender at J & J, must be rolling over in his grave when he sees that from up above."

"Too bad they never named that saloon 'Maloney's,' rather then the one in Delhi. For old time's sake let's stop by the Corner Pub; wait a minute, the sign says "Caritas." What a funny name for a saloon!"

Katie, the barmaid, told us that it's the name of the current owner's girlfriend. He has only had the bar about a month. Over the past several years, they have gone through a host of owners. I remembered when we used to come here on Friday nights. The place would be packed. Bob would be drawing another caricature of someone to hang on the wall. The place used to be just like the Cheers bar, right here in Price Hill. Everyone knew your name, or should I say your face, because it was hanging on the wall with a bunch of others. We had plenty of sock showers for guys getting married in the basement of this place. I remember the one little staircase leading up from that basement. I was sure glad there was never a fire down there.

"Well, Katie, we would like to stay and join in the Karaoke tonight, but Buddy will be heading back down south soon and my voice is not too good. And bedtime is ten o'clock. Here's hoping you have a good crowd, and good luck to the new owner."

"I see the fruit market that used to be on the corner of Glenway and Sidney is gone. I can remember the night he was getting ready to open. We helped him unload his truck with all the fruit. He promised us a watermelon for helping. Too bad you had to go and drop one, Buddy. Instead of taking our melon home, we had to stand on the corner eating the busted one. Later on, a butcher moved in with him. On Friday nights, he would fry fish and sell it by the pound. I think not only everyone from the Hill came for the fish, but I saw guys from firehouses clear across the city. It was not unusual to wait an hour or so for your fish."

As I looked over there at Western Hills High School, it brought back memories of when we were going to Elder. On a holy day, we would be off school and would make our way out to West High to see our friends Eb and Jim. "Remember that one day when Mr. Tower, the assistant principal, caught us in the hall and took us into Mr. Siehl's office, saying he caught us in the hall without a pass? We kept trying to explain we weren't students there. That didn't mean anything to him. We were in his school and we had violated his rules. Next thing, the guy that ran the woodshop showed up with a big paddle. We were told to bend over and Mr. Tower began to swing that paddle, five swings to each one of us. I couldn't sit down to eat for a week, but I never would tell my mom why. One thing for sure, on a holy day from thereafter, we went to church and forgot about West Hi!"

"What the heck has happened to West High's football field? It's shrunk. No more stands. I can remember when they used to play the Thanksgiving game there, when it was their turn," commented Buddy.

I chimed in that the West High band even had someone pulling the bass drum on wheels and they had old Don, the drum major, strutting down the field, throwing his baton over the

Western Hills High School football field back in the old days

goal post and catching it while everyone cheered. In those days catching the baton was almost more important than winning the game. And then, Elder's band would come out with about a dozen people and play their fight song.

"Buddy, do you know that after all those exciting games, the teams played their last game a couple of years ago? Kind of makes you feel a little sad."

"And they might have shrunk the football field, but they sure went hogwild on the baseball field, with bleachers behind home plate and all. In the summer they have a college level, wooden-bat team playing their games here with some good, young ballplayers. They also have different family nights where hot dogs are a buck. For a family, it gives them a chance to come out and see a good game without having to mortgage the house."

"Someone told me they went to one of the Reds' games on some free tickets. With parking, beer, and hot dogs they were lucky to get by spending fifty bucks. After a couple of beers, with beer at more than seven bucks a bottle, you're broke. I remember when we went to Crosley Field on Opening Day and sat in the field seats. It was so hot we used to buy a bucket of ten bottles of beer for ten bucks. Buddy, remember that day the guy tried to cheat us by turning several empty bottles upside down? Jessie grabbed that guy by the collar. All the other beer boys, along with their boss, came running. Jessie said the guy owed him five bucks. I thought for sure we were going to have to fight our way out, but the guy just handed Jessie five bucks back. I bet he never tried that trick again."

"Well Buddy, it looks like Philipps' Swimming Pool is still there, though they probaby won't open this year, I'm afraid. Remember how we would walk or thumb our way out from the front of the Hill on a Sunday afternoon? Usually we didn't have half-a-buck to go swimming, but watching Roy Hotchkiss and

Philipps' Swim Club on Glenway Avenue

his crew put on a diving show from the pavilion was well worth the trip. Big Herm would do his famous "cannonball" off the ten-foot board. He was extremely happy when he splashed water on all of us watching from above."

Fifty cents was a lot of money in those days to pay for swimming, so our swimming was done mostly in the river or Schulte's pond at West Eighth Street and Harris Avenue. A big sewer pipe ran right through the middle of the pond. I now wonder if the sewage was leaking into the pond. Oh well, we survived. If we had a spare quarter, we would walk over to Gehrum's on Queen City. It wasn't much bigger than some backyard pools today, but we sure had fun.

"Hey, look at that, a wrecker tearing down the building where Peggy's Grill used to be. It's really sad to see so many buildings being torn down. Boy, there will be a lot of teary eyes when they see Peggy's is gone. A lot of first dates were shared over a double-decker and a cherry Coke; we sure had some exciting times there. Remember all the sororities and fraternities that would hold their meetings at Peggy's? I can remember one special night. Remember that fraternity from West High? I think they called

147

themselves "TO's." They were not liked too well by guys from Elder, in fact many from West High didn't even like them. They were meeting there one night and one of their members drove a little Austin car. He really thought he was something with the girls. He would always park the car right in front of Peggy's so he could show off. We got together that night and picked the car up, carried it onto the sidewalk, and placed it in front of the door leading into Peggy's. No one could get in or out of the place. He tried to pass the keys out the front door for someone to move the car, but everyone told him they couldn't drive."

"Our friend's dad was a policeman and we wanted him to call his dad and have the car ticketed for parking on the sidewalk. That didn't happen, so finally the guy had to squeeze out the window and move the car himself. From then on he found a new parking space."

Moeller's Grill: "Look, even Moeller's Grill is gone. They replaced that with another strip mall. With the railroad yards just down the street, a bunch of railroaders would always be in there having a drink and telling their stories about work on the railroad. Again, even the railroad decided to pick up their tracks and go someplace else."

"Not that this has to do with anything, but do you remember George, the ballplayer? I remember he threw one of his fastballs by me one day and I think the ball was in the catcher's glove before I ever started to swing."

"Yeah, when you look at some of these ballplayers today and the salaries they are getting, you have to wonder. Guys like George were a lot better and never got the chance to move up to the majors, because of World War II."

Champions: "Well, Buddy, it has been a long day and I better get you something to eat before you head back to your wife. Let's just swing down Crookshank Road and stop at one of the places there."

"Crookshank, with restaurants? The only thing I can ever remember being on that street was the incinerator. Sure hope you aren't taking me there for a sandwich!"

"No, the incinerator is long gone. This is where the franchise bars are. We have a choice between Applebee's, O'Charley's, Champions, and Patrick's Sports Bar. Let's go into Champions. I haven't been in there for a long time; but the one thing you have to promise me is that you won't get tied up talking to an Elder grad. You see, Doc O'Connor runs the place and he has sons that are Elder boys. But, I think that most of the alumni that hang out here are of a younger vintage than we are. Sure glad there isn't a game on tonight because they've got about ten big screen TVs. Sometimes it's hard to know what game you are watching."

"Yeah, I know how that is, Froggy. One night I was in a bar watching a game and I saw a player running back a kickoff and, all of a sudden, I turned my head and on the other set a guy was intercepting a pass. Don't these people know that we old-timers have a slow reaction time and it takes us a while to focus?"

"By the way, the hamburger cost four and a half and it's not as good as the ones we used to get at Joe Brauer's for a half a buck. But that's life today, so eat up; I'm going to get you home in good condition tonight!"

"Well, here we are back to your place, Buddy. You be sure to tell your wife I watched over you today and made sure you didn't meet up with any of those old building trades buddies who got you all bleary-eyed last night."

"Well, old friend, we sure did have a fun few days."

"We did. You have a safe trip home to Florida and next time don't stay away so long. Maybe we can hit a few of the old drug stores we used to hang out at. I don't figure we can get into too much trouble there, although most of them do sell beer."

"Yeah, and maybe we can check out a few corner lots where we used to play ball, too. Well, see you later, Froggy!"

ABOUT THE AUTHOR

Larry Schmolt

L arry is a lifelong resident of Price Hill. He grew up on Purcell Avenue and attended Holy Family Grade School and Elder High School. After serving in the army during the Korean War and returning home to Cincinnati, he joined the Cincinnati Fire Department in 1952. That same year, he married Lee Sanzere. They settled in their home on Rutledge Avenue and raised three daughters. Today, Larry enjoys his ten grandchildren and continues to live in that same Rutledge Avenue home.

After retiring from the Fire Department in 1983 as an Assistant Fire Chief, Larry made a run at politics, but was unsuccessful in his bids for a seat on the Cincinnati City Council and in the Ohio State House of Representatives. He then concentrated his efforts locally and served for ten years as President of the Price Hill Civic Club. During that time, he was instrumental in helping to form the Price Hill Historical Society, which he conceived of in association with the celebration of the 75th anniversary of the Civic Club.

Larry is also a member of the Seton Council of the Knights of Columbus and was a past Grand Knight. He volunteers as a docent at the Fire Museum, and is a Pastoral Minister at The Christ Hospital. For the past five years, he has served as the Coordinator of the Price Hill Historical Society and Museum.

CPSIA information can be obtained at www.ICGtesting.com
263875BV00004B/5/P